MEXICO TRAILS

Your Adventure Guide to 43 Short Hikes & Walking Trails in Mexico

By

Gerry Recksiedler

Order this book online at www.trafford.com
or email orders@trafford.com

Most Trafford titles are also available at major online book retailers.

Note for Librarians: A cataloguing record for this book is available from Library
and Archives Canada at www.collectionscanada.ca/amicus/index-e.html

Printed in Victoria, BC, Canada.

ISBN: 978-1-4251-4086-1 (SC)

ISBN: 978-1-4251-4087-8 (E-BOOK)

*Our mission is to efficiently provide the world's finest, most comprehensive book publishing
service, enabling every author to experience success. To find out how to publish your
book, your way, and have it available worldwide, visit us online at www.trafford.com*

Trafford rev. 10/13/2009

 www.trafford.com

North America & international
toll-free: 1 888 232 4444 (USA & Canada)
phone: 250 383 6864 ♦ fax: 812 355 4082

CONTENTS

Acknowledgments

I wish to thank all those people who provided information or assistance in locating the trails described in this book. First of all I would like to thank my faithful traveling companion and wife Maureen for accompanying me on most of the trail explorations. I would especially like to thank those representatives who work in the Mexican government offices of El Instituto Nacional de Estadisticas, Geografia e Informatica (INEGI) located in the capital cities of the different states in which the trails are found. They were especially patient and helpful in assisting me to locate the necessary topographical maps and other materials required to identify and explore hiking areas in Mexico. I am also grateful to the many people of Mexico whom we met during the course of our trail explorations. They were always friendly and helpful, often giving us advice, and sometimes accompanying us on the trails.

I want to give a special thanks to Gerry Moore and Darryl Hall for taking the time to edit the book and for making many suggestions for improvement.

Disclaimer

As in any outdoor activity, there are inherent risks in walking trails in Mexico. In rough terrain all persons are advised to be aware of possible changes or hazards that can occur along any hiking trails due to the weather or human activity.

Due to the possibility of personal error, topographical error, misinterpretation of information, and the many changes both natural and man-made that can happen to any trail, *Mexico Trails*, the author, publisher, and all other persons or companies directly or indirectly associated with this publication assume no responsibility for accidents, injury, damage or any losses by individuals or groups using this publication.

Introduction

Mexico

Mexico is a crowded country. Its present population is approximately 100 million people. Roughly speaking, 15% are of European (mostly Spanish) descent; 60% are Mestizo (Spanish and Indian decent); and 25% are Indigenous. No matter where you go in Mexico you will almost always find people occupying the land. The majority of the people live in a band running east-west from Veracruz to Guadalajara. The further north you go from Mexico city, the less population pressure there is on the land.

Travelers in Mexico who find themselves off the beaten path may be met by curiosity or shyness by the locals. Generally speaking, most of the people that you will meet on the trails described in this book will be friendly or at the worst indifferent. Mexicans are generally friendly, humorous and want to be helpful to visitors. Language is the biggest barrier to friendly contact with the people. Some people may be shy or ignore you because they don't imagine that a conversation is possible. Knowing even a few words of Spanish goes a long way in breaking the ice. Often the local people will be very curious about you and will be full of questions.

Although Spanish is the main language of the country, there are still many native dialects spoken. Some of the indigenous people that you may run into on the trail may react cooly to your presence. After five centuries of exploitation, they have learned to be mistrustful of newcomers. The further south you go into the country, the more native Indian people you will encounter.

Geography

Mexico covers almost 2 million square kilometers and runs roughly in a north-west to south-east direction. Northern and central Mexico are generally mountainous. The country has two coastal plains on the east and west sides and two mountain ranges running roughly north-south: the Western Sierra Madre and the Eastern Sierra Madre. The Western Sierra Madre runs parallel to the Pacific coast for about 1,400 kilometers. The Eastern Sierra Madre runs down along the Gulf coast. The interior consists of a high central plateau known as the Altiplano Central. It varies in altitude, from between 1,000 to 2000 meters. The Altiplano itself is split up by smaller ranges. At about the same latitude as Mexico City lies a chain of volcanos and mountains running east and west across the country called the Eje Neovolcanico, including Mexico's highest peak, Pico de Orizaba. (5, 675 meters). Beyond the valley of Mexico City there are the Southern Sierra Madre mountains which run across the states of Guerrero and Oaxaca to the Pacific Ocean. From here the land flattens out in the Isthmus of Tehuantepec and the Yucatan Peninsula except for the high central plateau area of Chiapas.

The greater part of Mexico lies south of the Tropic of Cancer making it technically a "tropical" country. However, because much of its terrain reaches into the higher elevations, the weather can be anything but tropical. For example, the city of Puebla is at about 2,160 meters, Mexico City is at about 2,240 meters and Guadalajara is at about 1,500 meters. It can become quite cool at these elevations, especially at night. One day in mid-December of 1997 Guadalajara received several centimeters of snow. For further information on the climate, geology, flora and fauna of the country I would recommend reading Jim Conrad's book "Mexico: A hikers guide to Mexico's natural history" as these topics are beyond the scope of this book.

The majority of the trails in this book are found in the mountainous areas of Mexico which makes for spectacular hiking.

Further Information

Maps

Most of the trails described in this book are not signed, so follow the directions as described and ignore other trails that you may come upon. Most of the trails in Mexico are working trails used by the local people as routes of commerce and communication between villages or villages and farms. The maps and trails provided in this book were drawn up using 1:50,000 scale maps and a Global Positioning System unit (GPS) to provide coordinates along the tail. The complete maps are available from Mexican government map offices in the various state capital cities in the country: the Instituto Nacional de Estadisticas, Geografia e Informatica (INEGI). Their web   site is www.inegi.gob.mx. I've found that by visiting the local map office in the capital city of the state that you are in, it's easy to pick up the required maps. They also carry maps of the neighboring states. If you are going to be hiking trails in the next state as well, you can get the necessary maps for both states at the same office. I've found the people in the map offices to be extremely helpful. Also, maps are cheaper to purchase at these local offices rather than ordering them over the internet. It is possible to order maps over the internet, but it is not always easy.

The maps provided in this book show general views of the trails. Once you have decided to hike a trail in a particular area of the country, pick up the recommended detailed topographical map as greater detail will be needed than is provided here. The maps are not necessarily to scale. The maps and trail descriptions are intended to supplement the topographical maps by describing the trails, rating their difficulty and noting key intersections with other trails. Many of the trails described will not appear on the topographical maps. It is recommended that hikers take a GPS unit along with them in order to confirm their position on the topographical maps.

For all the maps in this book, North is always oriented up unless otherwise indicated.

What to take

Hikers' Checklist

The following is a checklist of useful items to have on the trail:

◆   Hiking boots or walking shoes (broken in).
◆   Rain gear (rainy season).
◆   Water bottle or bottled water.
◆   Water filter or purifying tablets.
◆   Long-sleeved shirt (sun protection).
◆   Long pants (sun and cactus prickle protection).
◆   Sunhat and sunglasses.
◆   Sunscreen.
◆   First-aid kit (bandages, tape, band-aids, antiseptic cream, tweezers, moleskin, aspirins, eye wash).
◆   Insect repellent.

- Compass, whistle, flashlight.
- Global Positioning System (GPS) unit.
- Day Pack.
- Swiss Army Knife.

It's recommended that one take a GPS along on every hike. As mentioned before, there are many trails running through the Mexican back country, some of which lead off from or intersect with the trails described in this book. As there are usually no trail markers or signage of any kind, it is easy to stray off the described trails. If, upon doing a GPS check, you should you find yourself off the described trail, it's a simple matter of backtracking or using the "Go To" function to get back to where you want to be. GPS hand held units are quite affordable and are coming down in price all the time. They are accurate to within +/- 3 to 5 meters. **Remember, the trails in Mexico are not like the trails that you find in the parks in the U.S. or Canada. Should you get lost, you're on your own. There are no park wardens to come looking for you.**

Hazards on the trail:

- Loose rock: Because many trails are used by the local campesinos to move their livestock from one place to another, the animals tend to stir up and loosen small rocks on the trail, especially on the steeper portions. This is where a good pair of hiking boots are needed for good grip and ankle support.

- Washouts and Bulldozers: Trail conditions can change radically from one year to the next because of washouts due to heavy rains during the rainy season or due to road construction. If you come upon an area where the trail becomes vague or difficult to follow, turn around and backtrack to your starting point rather than risk the possibility of getting lost or hurt due to altered terrain.

- Dogs: During your hikes you will encounter dogs that will do no more than bark at you. Generally, having a walking stick with you is enough to ward them off. Another trick is to pretend to pick up a stone and fake a throw. If that doesn't work then pick up a real stone and throw it. Mexican dogs are afraid of stones as the locals often use stones to chase off unwanted dogs.

- Snakes: Although one should always be aware that snakes may be on the trail, you will rarely see one. Snakes attack only when cornered or provoked, so give them a wide berth. Never put your hands under rocks or logs. Wearing good boots and thick socks will help. Most snakes become active at night, so if you are still hiking into the late evening or into the night, be extra cautious.

- Scorpions: Even though scorpions become aggressive only when disturbed, don't stick your hands around rocks, logs, sticks, boards, etc. unless you can see clearly there is nothing hiding under them.

- Water: Don't depend on finding drinking water along the trail. Never drink water from a stream no matter how clean it may appear. Most surface water sources will be polluted due to the fact that domestic animals and human activity can be found almost anywhere in Mexico, even at higher altitudes. If necessary, a water filter or water purifying tablets can be used to make water safe for drinking. In the dry season most streams dry up completely. Always take a sufficient amount of purified or bottled water with you and avoid the risk of having to drink water from dubious sources.

♦ Cactus: There are various types of cacti, some with large firm barbs and others with soft fuzzy ones. The soft fuzzy ones are the ones that can be the most difficult to remove from your body. They are like tiny hairs and can be difficult to see. They can penetrate through light clothing and into the skin. This is where a pair of tweezers can come in handy. Cello or masking tape can be used to remove the fuzzy barbs. **Be careful where you sit or go to the bathroom.**

♦ Dehydration: When walking at higher altitudes and in warm temperatures, one can become dehydrated very quickly. As mentioned above, wear light fabric long-sleeved shirts and pants as well as a wide brimmed hat for sun protection. Also, bring plenty of water and drink often to keep up your fluids.

♦ Heat exhaustion: Overexertion in high temperatures can lead to heat exhaustion. Symptoms of heat exhaustion are feeling faint, nauseous, a rapid heartbeat, cold and clammy skin, and pale colour in the face. Any of these symptoms suggest that you should take a rest in a cool shady place and drink liquids to replenish your fluids. Eating some high energy snacks is good as well.

♦ Hypothermia: Because some of the walks are at higher altitudes and somewhat exposed, there exists the possibility of experiencing hypothermia. Because the days are warm, one is tempted to bring only light clothing. However, when hiking up steep trails, one tends to sweat and clothing can get wet. Wetness along with wind in exposed areas can cause rapid evaporation and cooling causing a sudden drop in body temperature. Also, when the sun begins to dip behind a mountain in the late afternoon or evening, the air temperature can suddenly dip and conditions can become much cooler. Always carry a light sweater and a windproof/waterproof shell. A gortex jacket is a good type of outer garment to take along on any hike for emergency use.

How to use this book
If you are just a beginner hiker or just want some gentle walking, then try those trails classed as "easy". For hikes of less than a full day you can always just walk a couple of hours down the trail and then return on the same trail. Experienced hikers should be able to do any of the trails described in this book keeping in mind the season, weather conditions and the altitude.

Hikers' Code

Most tourists that I have encountered on our walks in different parts of the world generally are good about staying on the trail, leaving domestic and wild animals alone and not littering. People rambling over the Mexican countryside should be aware that at times the terrain can become rugged and dangerous. Hikers should always give themselves enough time to do the walk, not over extend themselves and not try to hike trails that are beyond their abilities.

♦ Leave all gates as you find them, whether it looks like there is a farm or ranch there or not. Many Mexican farmers live in small towns or villages but have an area of land fenced off in the surrounding hills or mountains where they allow their animals to roam or pasture. It may also be an area that they want to keep domestic animals from entering and causing damage.

♦ Never walk over cultivated land. Fruit and other corps are someone's private property and should not be touched.

♦ Pack out what you pack in. Take all your litter with you.

♦ Walk quietly through all villages and towns. Dogs will often bark at you. Ignore them but should a dog appear menacing, don't hesitate to display your walking stick to the dog.

♦ Leave domestic animals alone. Any cattle, horses, donkeys or goats that you encounter are not tame. Making loud noises or trying to touch or photograph them may cause them to run in fear and hurt themselves. Often they are semi-wild and could be dangerous.

♦ Take plenty of water as it can get quite hot during the day.

♦ Do not take risks. Do not attempt to walk beyond your capacity and do not wander off the trails.

♦ Do not walk alone. Always tell a responsible person exactly where you are going and when you expect to return. Remember, if you become lost or injured, it may be a long time before you are found. Be sure to take a GPS, compass, first-aid kit, whistle, flashlight, extra water and warm clothing - as well as some high energy food.

Hiking Time

The times given to do each of the day hikes listed are ample and include several breaks. Maureen and I have walked all the routes described in this book and she always makes sure that we stop often enough to enjoy the surroundings, especially when I am hell bent to go further on down the trail. The trails described herein offer a tremendous amount of beauty and one should slow down to appreciate the surroundings. Always remember that when hiking in hilly or steep terrain, it takes at least twice as long to go up than it takes to come back down.

GPS Readings
Most of the GPS co-ordinates given in this book are in metric units (Northings and Eastings) to correspond to the topographical maps from the INEGI map offices. Occasionally coordinates are given in Longitude and Latitude units as there are a few maps that are only available in that format.

Map Legend

Paved Road	▬▬▬	Fence Line	··········
Dirt/Gravel Road	– – – – ·	Electrical Line	· · · · · ·
Two Track Trail	= = = = :	Gate	❚
Described Trail	– – – – –	Building	■
Viewpoint	✸	Trail Routes	Ⓣ
Other Trails	· · · · · · ·	Campground	△
Contour and Elevation	⌒1700⌒		

State of Nuevo Leon

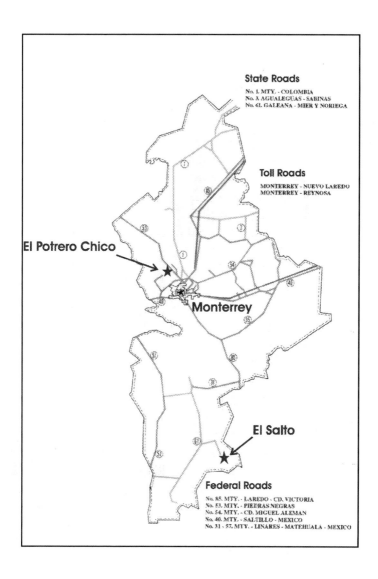

State Roads

No. 1. MTY. - COLOMBIA
No. 3. AGUALEGUAS - SABINAS
No. 61. GALEANA - MIER Y NORIEGA

Toll Roads

MONTERREY - NUEVO LAREDO
MONTERREY - REYNOSA

El Potrero Chico

Monterrey

El Salto

Federal Roads

No. 85. MTY. - LAREDO - CD. VICTORIA
No. 53. MTY. - PIEDRAS NEGRAS
No. 54. MTY. - CD. MIGUEL ALEMAN
No. 40. MTY. - SALTILLO - MEXICO
No. 31 - 57. MTY. - LINARES - MATEHUALA - MEXICO

El Potrero Chico Recreation Area

El Potrero Chico is located just on the south west edge of the town of Hidalgo which in turn is located approximately 40 km north of the city of Monterrey. Take either the toll road or the free road which arcs around the northern outskirts of Monterrey and then take Highway 53 north to Hidalgo and Monclova. As you approach the town of Hidalgo, you will see the Sierra San Miguel mountains rising on the west side of the highway and a cleft in the mountains which is the entrance way to a beautiful valley ringed by mountains. This cleft is called Boca (mouth) de Potrero Chico. Just past km 28 as you enter the town, the highway branches off to the right. At this point watch for the Bienvenido Hidalgo sign. The approach into town basically goes straight on along a divided boulevard with street lights running down the middle. Shortly you will come to a small roundabout and a Bital bank on the left. At the roundabout there is a directional sign for El Potrero Chico. Turn left here and follow the directional signs through the town heading in the general direction of the cleft in the mountain.

El Potrero Chico Trails Locator Map

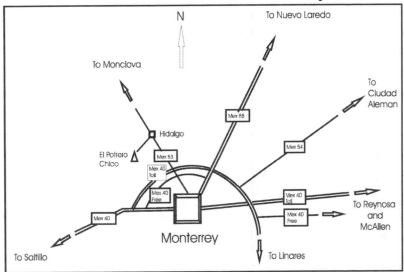

14

There are a couple of campgrounds located just on the south-west edge of town near the cleft which can be used as a base for all the hikes in this area. Two of our favorite camp grounds are Homero's campgound or Cerro Gordo campground. Rock climbers from all over the world come here to climb the rock walls located at the entrance way to the valley. When we visited the area for the first time we were fortunate enough to have lucked into a pig roast with beer hosted by Homero, the local Mexican campground operator, and had the opportunity to rub shoulders with rock climbers from Mexico, U.S., Canada and Europe. A group from Minnesota graciously offered to include us in their climb the next day. We politely declined the offer.

Gateway to El Potrero Chico

Route 1: Del Luminati Wall Trail

Time: A leisurely 5 hour hike including a lunch stop
Distance: 10 km. return from campground
Difficulty: Moderate
Hazards: Some loose rock on trail; cow pies
Elevation Change: 300 meters
Topo Maps: Hidalgo G-14-C-15 Nuevo Leon

This trail is located in a natural amphitheater which has lovely mountain views, some bird life and interesting flora. You are unlikely to become disoriented as the entrance way to the amphitheater is visible most of the time. From Homero's camp ground [14R0352061; UTM 2871489] walk south towards the pass through the rock wall. Start by walking south on the paved road that leads to the pass. In about 1 km you will pass by a Welcome sign and what appears to be a recreation area on the right-hand side of the road. This is the point where you will probably see rock climbers pasted up against the rock walls moving very slowly and carefully upwards. Soon the road changes to dirt. Within ½ km there is a Texas gate cattle crossing. The dirt road then crosses a wash (usually dry in the dry season).

Next you will see two sets of dirt tracks branching off to the right. Ignore them. At 700 m past the Texas gate you will pass a sign identifying private property called "Los Pirules". There is a house on the property. About 200 m past the Los Pirules sign there is a branch in the road [14R 0352103; UTM 2869759]. Take the right branch which heads west between two fence lines. About 300 m up this dirt track you come to another branch [14R0351715; UTM 2869580]. The left branch heads towards two concrete block structures. Continue straight ahead on the right branch. Follow the dirt track straight ahead for about another 400 m until you come to a metal gate {14R 0351363; UTM 2869585]. Pass through or around this gate. Within another 250 m the dirt track skirts up next to a hogsback on the left hand side of the trail. At this point there is another fork in the trail [14R 0351050; UTM 2869565]. Take the right fork and head towards the concrete building visible ahead and on the right. (From the branch off the main dirt road there is the occasional post on the right hand side of the dirt track that has red paint sprayed on the top.) In about another 500 m the track drops down, crosses a dry arroyo (stream), then heads up hill to the right.

At this point look for a foot path branching off to the left and following along the right side of the arroyo. Watch for rocks arranged to outline the footpath and rock cairns to mark the trail. There are many paths along here created by cattle so it is important to keep to the trail that is outlined from time to time with rocks. Within a few minutes the footpath drops down and follows the dry rocky stream bed for about 20 meters. The footpath then branches off to the left out of the stream bed. It can be easily missed so watch carefully here for the path branching off. The footpath follows along the left-hand side of the arroyo, then crosses it and follows along the right-hand side. The climb is gradual but steady.

As you progress, you will come to a point along the trail opposite a rock overhang on your right [14R 0350250; UTM 2869786]. Further on the foot path crosses a dry stream bed and begins to swing south [14R 0350060; UTM 2869746]. You are now approximately 1.75 km from where you left the dirt track and picked up the foot path. In about another 125 m, if you look up to the right, you will see a hole in a rock outcrop[14R 0349952; UTM 2869624].

During your progress along this stretch of the hike you will be noticing two hills on your left. After having crossed the stream bed for the third time you will come up close to the second hill. In another 150 m you will encounter a series of switchbacks [14R 0350095; UTM 2869375] which lead you up and around the second hill continuing in a westerly direction and then south until you come to what appears to be a small saddle [14R 0350039; UTM 2869339]. This is the highest point in the hike with a beautiful 360 degree view of the valley ringed by mountains.

This is a good place to stop for lunch and enjoy the views. From here the trail descends around the hill, first in a southerly direction and then in an easterly direction. The trail is a little vague at first due to the disturbance by cattle; however, after about 20 m it becomes distinct again, first with a short climb and then it begins descending rapidly. Watch for red paint on the occasional rock along the trail [14R 0350090; UTM 2869169]. Pay special attention along this stretch as the trail becomes vague from time to time. About 500 m down the trail from the viewpoint, the trail crosses some exposed flat rock [14R 0350550; UTM 2868891]. Within another 500 m the trail crosses another dry stream bed which then runs south of and parallel to the trail. A short distance beyond, the trail becomes a dirt track again [14R0350936; UTM 2868862] which descends in an easterly direction around the hills on your left.

About 2 km from the viewpoint look for what appears to be a sinkhole just off to the right of the dirt track. A little further on you will notice three white concrete markers running more or less in a north-south direction [14R 0351619; UTM 2868758]. A bit further on, if you look into what looks like an old gravel pit on the right-hand side of the dirt track you can see a large iron frame which was probably used for gravel mining purposes sometime in the past. The track now descends steeply around a small hill on the left and comes out where the stream bed crossed the main dirt road which leads further into the valley. At this point turn left and follow the main dirt road north past Rancho los Panchos towards the pass through the rock wall to return to the campground.

View of valley from Viewpoint

Route 2: Loma La Gongora Trail

Time: A short day hike
Distance: 4 km return from trail head on the main valley road (dirt) or 12 km return from the campground
Difficulty: Moderate to strenuous
Hazards: Loose rock; dogs at mine site; cattle along trail
Elevation Change: 360 meters (from trail head); 540 meters (from campground)
Topo Maps: Hidalgo G-14-C-15 Nuevo Leon

This trail offers an interesting hike along a stream and past a working mine. The trailhead is located about 4 km from the campground on the main dirt road that runs south from the portal and then south-west into the valley. You have the option of walking from the campground to the trailhead (a distance of 4.6 km from Homero's campground) and then ascending the trail or driving from the campground to the trailhead. The main dirt road is normally passable for a standard vehicle. The road goes south through the portal and then at 3.2 km from the campground it makes a sharp 90 degree turn to the east. After the 90 degree bend in the road you will cross two significant stream crossings (usually dry in the dry season). Just after crossing the second dry streambed [14R 0352661; UTM 2868286] you will notice a dirt road turning off to the right (4.3 km from the campground) into a pleasant park-like area with a small dam which regulates water flow. Do not take this trail. Go on further for about 300 meters. You will notice a well used dirt road which branches off in a southerly direction [14R 0352902; UTM 2868027]. This is the road that leads to the mine site. Park here and begin walking. Do not attempt to drive up this road as there is a gate part way up the road and it is difficult to turn around at that point.

From the trailhead walk up the road that leads to the mine site. In about 1 km you will come to a gate [14R 0352650; UTM 2867785]. Pass through the gate and continue walking up the road until you come to the mine site [14R O352346: UTM 2867412]. The road ends here. Be aware that there may be dogs at the site. At the south end of the mine site you will pick up a well used trail which continues up along the east side of the stream bed. In about 500 meters you will come to a branch in the trail [14R 0351926; UTM2867232]. Take the right branch. Within a few minutes the trail will cross over to the west side of the stream and continue upwards. The trail gradually becomes more difficult with some loose rock and short switchbacks. Eventually the trail diminishes into what looks like a series of wandering goat tracks on a steep slope [14R 0351846; UTM 2866630]. At this point you have the option of scrambling on or turning around and returning back to the trailhead on the same trail.

Valley view from Loma La Gongora Trailhead

Route 3: Puerto El Zorrillo and Canada El Abra Trail.

Time: An all day hike
Distance: 8 km return from the trailhead on the main valley road (dirt) or 16 km return from the campground
Difficulty: Moderate to strenuous
Hazards: Loose rock on switchbacks; cattle on lower part of trail
Elevation Change: 360 meters (from trail head); 540 meters (from campground).
Topo Maps: Hidalgo G-14-C-15 Nuevo Leon

This trail offers some great views of the valley. The trailhead is located 4.8 km from the campground on the dirt road that runs south from the portal and then south west into the valley. One can walk from the campground to the trailhead or do as we did - drive from the campground and park at the trail head and save your energy for the haul up to Puerto El Zorrillo and the Canada El Abra valley. If you come to a fairly substantial metal gate on the main dirt road that looks like its meant to keep vehicles out, you've gone too far. Backtrack a few hundred meters and take the dirt road to the right that branches off the main dirt road [14R 0352908; UTM 2867867].

Although the beginning of the dirt road appears drivable at first glance, don't attempt to drive up because as one advances up the road, it becomes quite rough and suitable only for four wheel drive vehicles. A short while into the walk you will come to a gate [14R 0352988; UTM 2867655]. Pass through the gate and continue up the road which

19

Maureen and dog Lindi on trail with gateway to El Potrero Chico in Background

eventually crosses a stream descending out of the mountains on your right. Once across the stream the trail bends around to the right [14R 0353136; UTM 2867119] and then follows the stream for about 1 km. Up to this point the hike is fairly moderate. From here the trail leaves the stream and becomes a series of switchbacks [14R 0352601; UTM 2866975] until the pass at Puerto El Zorrillo is reached [14R 0352504; UTM 2866821].

From the pass one can get some magnificent views of the valley. Once on top, it's a pleasant walk through the Canada El Abra along a path that is easy to follow. Its mostly open country offering scenic views of the mountains on either side. The trail now descends gradually down the Canada El Abra valley. About ½ km beyond the top you will see a line of posts running across the landscape, probably the remains of an old fence line[14R 0352555; UTM2866653]. About 1 km further on there is a small corral and the ruins of a house on the left-hand side of the trail [14R 0351823; UTM 2865568]. A short distance further on you will find a few big trees offering some welcome shade - a good place to stop and rest before returning to the trailhead.

Although the trail continues in a southerly direction down the valley, it has not been checked out by us. According to the topo maps the trail continues to descend first gradually and then rather quickly down the other side of the mountain through a steep ravine to the flatlands on the other side of the mountain range.

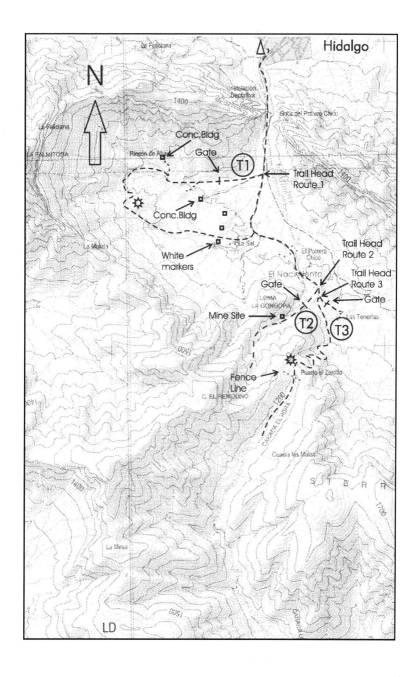

Hidalgo

N

Conc.Bldg
Gate
(T1)
Trail Head
Route 1

Conc.Bldg

White
markers

Trail Head
Route 2

Trail Head
Route 3

Gate
Mine Site
(T2)
Gate
(T3)

Fence
Line

El Salto Recreation Area

El Salto is located about 300 km by road south of Monterrey. The best approach by car is to take the north by-pass (Route 40) around the northern outskirts of Monterrey towards Saltillo. Before getting to Saltillo, take Route 57 which by-passes Saltillo to the east and head south for about 130 km until you come to the junction of Route 58 to Galeana and Linares. Turn east and drive for 33 km where you will come to the junction of Route 61. Drive south on Route 61 for about 80 km till you come to the town of La Escondida. This portion of the drive has beautiful scenery and the traffic is light. Turn east at La Escondida on a paved road which takes you through the towns of Aramberri and Zaragoza. Once

El Salto Trails Locator Map

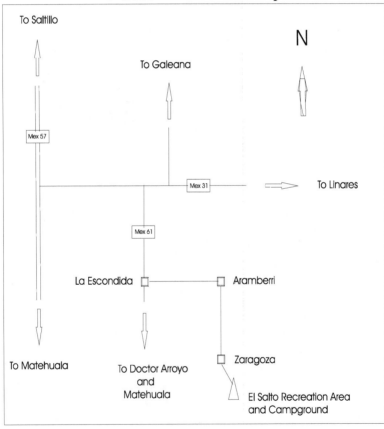

through Zaragoza, follow the signs to El Salto (3 km south of Zaragoza). Basically you drive to the end of the road until you come to the recreation area and the campsite. Allow yourself about 7 hours to drive from Monterrey to El Salto. Although the distance is only 300 km, once you get off Route 57 the roads are narrow and windy (although all are paved) and it is necessary to slow down and take care. But, what's the rush. You're here to relax and enjoy, right?

The El Salto Recreation Area is a beautiful spot to spend a few days hiking and relaxing. It has camping and picnic facilities, restrooms, and cabins although they are basic . This whole area is surrounded by magnificent mountains just made for hiking. Here you will find the beautiful 10 meter high "El Salto" waterfall, with its pools in shades of blue and green. You will also find another waterfall known as "Velo de Novia", named after its resemblance to a brides veil.

Route 4: Cierro La Nieve

Time: 8 hours return
Distance: 12 km return from campground
Difficulty: Leisurely, then strenuous
Hazards: Boulder hopping along stream; loose rocks on switchbacks
Elevation Change: 960 meters (1500 to 2460 meters)
Topo Maps: F-14-A-17 Nuevo Leon - Tamaulipas
Attractions: Views of the falls; visit a trout hatchery; hike along a stream with beautiful, tall deciduous trees; great views of the El Salto canyon

Starting at the campground [N 23 56.852' ;W 99 45.858'], walk up the path that goes along the left-hand side of the stream. Within a kilometer you will pass the trout fish hatchery. Just beyond the fish hatchery you will pass by two water conduits (a large one and a smaller one) coming from a water flow control tank located in the stream [N 23 56.563'; W 99 45.756']. Crawl through the hole in the metal fence by the control tank. From here the trail basically follows the stream for about 1.6 km.

This part of the walk is very pleasant and interesting with tall trees and opportunities to bathe in the pools found along the stream. As the canyon narrows you may have to climb over and around some boulders. Keep an eye on the left side of the stream and watch for a path that will ascend the left bank to bypass the large boulders in the stream.

Once past the boulders, the path begins to ascend upwards along a cliff facing the mountain on the opposite side [N 23 55.842'; W 99 45.852']. This is a good place to pause and enjoy the view before attempting the next portion of the trail. Beyond here the real work begins with the trail turning into a series of steep switchbacks [N 23 55.710' ; W 99 45.823'] ascending the west facing slope of Cierro La Nieve. Loose rock along the switchbacks makes for poor footing. There are not many opportunities for views until you begin emerging near the top.

The trail comes out at a fence line[N 23 55.217'; W 99 45.460'], then turns to the right and follows the fence line in a southerly direction. At this point you will have climbed approximately 750 meters in elevation up from the stream. Another fence line comes up from the south, then both fences turn in a south-easterly direction and run parallel to each

El Salto Waterfall

other creating a corridor along which the path continues. This portion of the trail was not checked out by us. Return to the campground via the same trail.

Route 5: Cierro Los Toros

Time: 7 hours
Distance: 6 km return
Difficulty: Moderate
Hazards: Some loose rock on trail
Elevation Change: 500 meters
Topo Maps: F-14-A-17 Nuevo Leon - Tamaulipas
Attractions: Great views of the town of Zaragoza in the valley, the El Salto Canyon and the upper El Salto valley

The trail begins about 20 meters east of the camp site booth at the entrance to the recreation area [N 23 56.825' ; W 99 45.960'] and begins to climb gradually. Within about 200 meters the trail passes through a gate and a fence line. The trail forks here. Take the trail that goes up to the left. Avoid the trail that goes down to the right. Shortly you will encounter some long and gradual switchbacks [N 23 56.860' ; W 99 45.963']. The footing is generally good.

About 1 km up the trail, you will come to a viewpoint [N 23 56.613' ; W 99 45.863'] which offers an expansive view of the town of Zaragoza and the valley. About 200 meters further on there is a branch in the trail [N 23 56.605' ; W 99 45.838']. The main trail goes to the right. About 50 meters ahead the trail splits again. Keep right. The trail now becomes covered with loose stones which makes walking a little more difficult. From here you start to get good views of El Salto Canyon.

Within the next kilometer the trail continues to switchback in a nice steady climb through open woods allowing views of the valley. Shortly thereafter the trail becomes steeper with more loose rock underfoot making walking a little more tricky. You will now come to a fork in the trail [N 23 56.175' ; W 99 46.156']. Take the right fork. The left fork is just a shortcut and joins the main trail immediately above.

About 2 km into the hike you will come to a viewpoint overlooking El Salto Canyon [N 23 56.145' ; W 99 46.090']. From here one can see the switchbacks of Route 3 up to Cierro El Nieve. From this point the trail climbs a bit more and then levels out and follows along the edge of the mountain at about the 2000 meter contour line. There is some up and down but nothing serious. In the third kilometer one gets some beautiful views of the upper El Salto valley [N 23 55.523' ; W 99 46.040']. We only explored about 3 km up this trail from the trailhead before turning around to return to the campground. The trail does continue on up the valley. One of the workmen at the campsite said that this trail goes on to a ranch - a distance of about 17 km one way. This has not been confirmed by us.

Cierro Los Torros trail along El Salto canyon

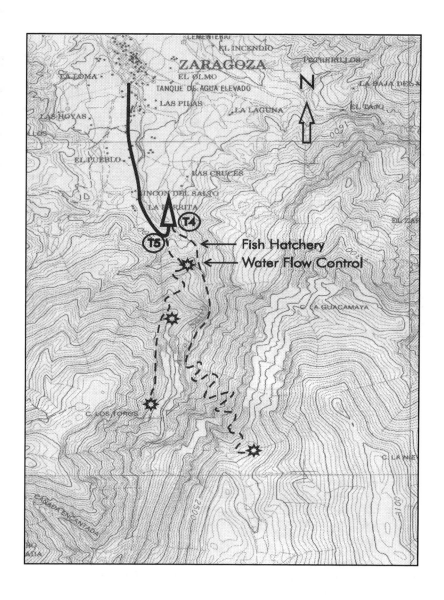

Fish Hatchery

Water Flow Control

State of Veracruz

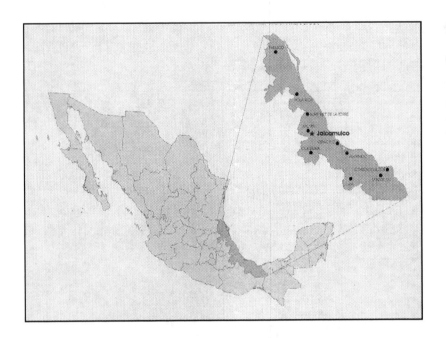

Jalcomulco

This area provides lots of options for day hikes. It is a beautiful area with low mountains and lots of green vegetation. The town of Jalcomulco can be accessed by road by driving (or taking a bus) about 10 km south from the city of Xalapa to Coatepec and then east about 30 km to Jalcomulco. Jalcomulco itself is a small sleepy little town located in the Los Pescados river valley. Here you will see the local people still using burros and horses to travel the trails and work the fields. This town is the favorite haunt of river rafters and kayakers from the U.S. and Canada. There are several companies set up here to cater to these activities. It's also possible to rent bicycles in town (near the bridge at the south end of town) or from one of the rafting companies if they are not being used by their own clients. As far as we could see there was no real accommodation available in the town for the drop-in tourist.

As there is regular bus service from Coatepec and Xalapa to Jalcomulco, one could stay in one of these locations and take the bus to Jalcomulco to do the hikes. If you have your own camper (preferably a smaller unit), you could camp along the south bank of the river just below and to the left of the bridge that crosses the river south of town.

All the trails described here are the actual trails used by the people working in the hills on their farms. They often travel out from the town and small surrounding villages in the morning on their burros and return in the evening. In every case, when we met the campesinos, they were very friendly and helpful when asked for directions. In one case a group of campesinos riding burros led us down one of the trails to show us the way back to Jalcomulco.

Jalcomulco Trails Locator Map

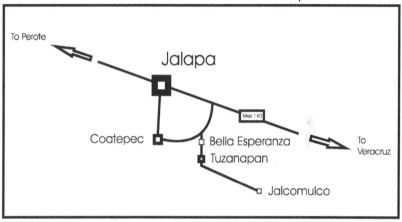

Route 6: Jalcomulco to Buenavista (Circle Trip)

Time: An all day hike
Distance: 12 km return from the bridge
Difficulty: Moderate
Hazards: Some loose rocks on the switchbacks
Elevation Change: 300 meters
Topo Maps: E-14-B-37 Coatepec

Starting at the bridge which crosses the Los Pescados River at the south end of town, cross the bridge to the south side of the river [14Q 0734980; UTM 2138617]. Turn right and follow the dirt road that heads in a south-westerly direction. Shortly after crossing a small stream that flows into the river [14Q 0734770; UTM 2138619], the trail splits off from the road to the right and begins to climb. The road parallels the trail on the left for a few hundred meters before stopping. It appeared that the road was under construction when we were there. In about 1 km from the bridge you will come to a viewpoint which overlooks the river and the town [14Q 0734439; UTM 2138269]. A few hundred meters further on you will come to a branch in the trail where there is a "Rio y Montana" sign nailed up on a mango tree [14Q 0734265; UTM 2138200]. The right branch leads back down to the river via a set of concrete steps and eventually to a trail heading upstream along the south side of the river. Take the trail that branches to the left. Within 50 meters you will come to another branch in the trail. Branch left again and follow the red arrow way markers.

For the next kilometer or so the trail begins to gently switchback through the mango trees affording some beautiful views of Jalcomulco and the river valley. Eventually the trail reaches the top of the escarpment and flattens out [14Q 0734263; UTM 2137412]. You will notice an electrical power line to the right. Here the vegetation changes abruptly to tall grass and shrubs. Very shortly a minor trail branches off to the left. Keep right on the main trail where you will see a mango tree way marked with red and blue paint. Within ½ km you will come to another fork in the trail [14Q 0733833; UTM 2137142]. Take the left fork which goes in a southerly direction towards Buenavista. In about 1 km the trail drops down through a ravine, crosses a stream bed and then climbs up the other side [14Q 0733722; UTM 2136377]. Once out of the ravine the trail continues on for another ½ km to a junction where four trails meet [14Q 0733948; UTM 2135936]. There is a fence on the left-hand side with blue paint on one of the posts. Go straight on (south) to Buenavista which is about ½ km ahead.

This little village is a good place to stop for a rest and perhaps buy a cold drink at the local tienda. The local church is worth a visit. The lady at the tienda said that there are some ruins about a half hour walk down the dirt road that comes into the village from the south-west. We did not check out the ruins due to time constraints.

From Buenavista backtrack to the junction of the four trails and the fence post with the blue paint as a way marker. At this point take the right branch which travels in an easterly direction following a fence line for a time. In about ½ km the fence line runs out. At this

View of valley from trail to Buenavista

point you will come to a post and another trail running north-south which intersects with the main trail [14Q 0734546; UTM 2136139]. Continue heading straight on in an easterly direction. A couple of hundred meters further on you will come to another fence line on the left-hand side of the trail. Continue on for about 200 meters where the fence line comes to an end and there is an open gate. The trail now follows through the shrubs for about 100 meters until you pick up another fence line on the right-hand side of the trail. At this point the trail and the fence line head first in a north-easterly and then in an easterly direction [14Q 0735026; UTM 2136605].

About 1 km from the open gate, you will come to another trail junction at a mango tree [14Q0735904; UTM 2136819]. At this point trees of any size are rare, so the mango tree should stand out. The main trail continues straight on in an easterly direction. **Do not take this trail**. Take the trail that branches to the left (north-easterly) at the mango tree. Within 200 meters you will come to two more trail intersections - first one coming in from the left, then another coming in from the right. Keep walking straight ahead (northerly). Next you will see a fence and a post [14Q 0736061; UTM 2137134]. Continue straight ahead (northerly). Within a kilometer the trail comes to the edge of the escarpment overlooking the river valley [14Q 0736426; UTM 2137837]. Here the trail begins to descend quite rapidly back into the river valley through mango trees via a series of switchbacks for about 1.5 km. Watch for blue way markers along the trail. This is quite a pretty part of the trail and it's in reasonably good shape. Eventually the trail exits onto the dirt road [14Q 0735701; UTM 2138335] that runs east from Jalcomulco down the river valley. Turn left (west) and follow the dirt road back to Jalcomulco.

Route 7: Jalcomulco to Apazapan and Coetzala

Time: An all day hike
Distance: 12 km return via Apazapan; 17 km return via Coetzala
Difficulty: Easy to Moderate.
Hazards: Some large boulders and stones on trail on south side of river; road traffic on paved road on north side of river
Elevation Change: 180 meters
Topo Maps: E-14-B-37 Coatepec
Attractions: Bring swim gear (optional)

Note: This hike consists of a shorter loop through Apazapan with the option of doing a longer loop through Coetzala.

This hike starts on the east side of town. From the center of town take the street that's paved with stone and has two concrete tracks heading east. This street leads to a paved road on the east side of the town [14Q 0735498; UTM 2138914] heading east to Apazapan and Coetzala. In the first 3 km the road gradually climbs to its highest point on the route to offer views of Apazapan and the Los Pescados river. A small shrine is located at this point [14Q 0737976; UTM 2138635]. From here the road descends down to Apazapan. A school is located at the west end of the town [14Q 0739339; UTM

Los Pescados River

21382178]. There is a dirt road heading up to the left (north) for about 300 meters to an alberca (small swimming pool). This would be a good place to stop for a dip before carrying on. The main route continues straight on into the town of Apazapan. From the school walk about 1 km into the center of the town and then turn right towards the river to find the swinging bridge over the Los Pescados river [14Q0739462; UTM 2137613]. At this point you could return to Jalcomulco via the trail heading off to the right (upstream) on the south side of the river. **The directions for the return portion of the shorter walk back to Jalcamulco appears later on in this trail description.**

Those wishing to carry on to Coatzala can do so via the road that connects Apazapan to Coatzala along the north side of the river. It's about 2 km from Apazapan to Coatzala via the road. The road comes to an end at the north side of the river. From here you have to cross the swinging bridge over the river to Coatzala [14Q 0741556; UTM 2136862].

After crossing the bridge, look for the first street (trail)that comes in from the right (south). This street leads you south out of the town and eventually on to a foot and burro path that shortly swings to the east along the south side of the river leading back to Apazapan. About ½ km from Coatzala the trail branches [14Q0741374; UTM 2136517]. Take the right branch that follows the river. The left branch leads to a small farm. Within another ½ km you will come to another fork in the trail [14Q 0741117; UTM 2136575]. Take the right fork which follows along a barbed-wire fence. Continue on for another1.5 km. At this point you will come upon a trail coming in (merging) from the hills on the left (south) [14Q 0739593; UTM 2137056]. Continue straight ahead in an easterly to north-easterly direction. 50 meters further on, another trail merges from the hills on the left (south). Again, continue straight ahead (east) and pass through a gate. From here you can see Apazapan and the swinging bridge crossing from the town to the south side of the river. Within ½ km from here you will come upon a third trail running between two fence lines merging from the hills on the left (south) [14Q 0739544; UTM 2137378]. Again, continue straight ahead until you come out at the swinging bridge at Apazapan.

Those opting to do the shorter walk from Jalcomulco to Apazapan and return to Jalcomulco via the swinging bridge and the trail on the south side of the river can pick up the trail description here. This portion of the trail between Apazapan and the dirt road leading back to Jalcomulco is quite stony. Once across the swinging bridge from Apazapan, turn right (east). About 1.5 km east of the swinging bridge there is a wooden gate and a branch in the trail [14Q 073880; UTM 2137758]. One trail branches left (south) away from the river and up into the hills. Don't take this one. Proceed east along the river. From this point the trail basically follows along between two fence lines. About 1 km further along the trail comes to a T-junction [14Q 0738181; UTM 2137922]. One trail heads down to the right towards the river. Take the main trail that heads straight on in an easterly direction (up river). Within a ½ km you will come to another wooden gate [14Q 0737840; UTM 2138125]. Pass through the wooden gate and continue on for about another ½ km where the trail passes through a fence line which is open for passage [14Q 0737508; UTM 2138387]. Within the next 1 km the trail begins to climb rapidly until it joins with the dirt road coming from Jalcomulco [14Q 0737163;UTM 2138376]. At this point there are some great views of Apazapan and the river. At this juncture turn right and follow the dirt road east which gradually descends for about 2.5 km to Jalcomulco.

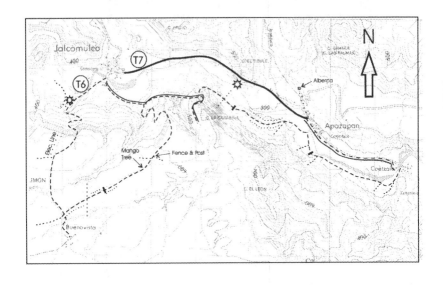

Queretaro State

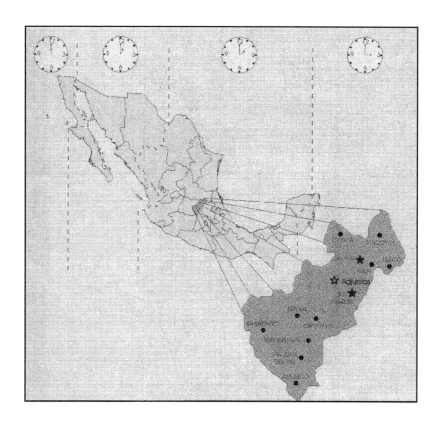

North-east Queretaro

The north-eastern portion of the state of Queretaro offers some interesting day hiking possibilities. To access this area by road, take the main highway (Mex 57) east of the city of Queretaro for about 19 km., then turn north on to Mex 4 to Bernal and Higuerillas. The trip up to Bernal takes you through some interesting agricultural country. Once past Bernal the character of the land changes to a dryer and more mountainous landscape. Shortly after Higuerrillas you will come to the junction of Mex 120.

North-East Queretaro State Trails Locator Map

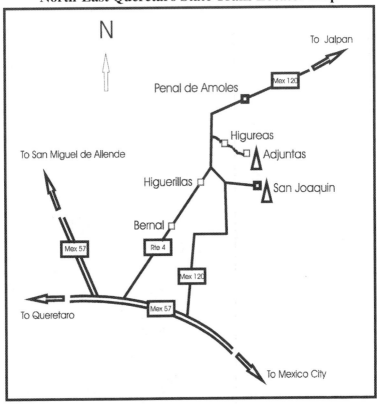

Road Access to Adjuntas: Turn left and go north for another 9 km. Here you should see a sign advertising Balneario El Oasis on the right hand side of the highway. Turn right (south) here and follow the dirt road into a village. The road crosses a dry stream bed called Arroyo Higuerillas, switches back through the village and then climbs up the other side. Continue on this road which follows along the arroyo for another 2 km until you come to another dirt road turning off to the left and down towards the stream bed. The main road continues on to the village of Adjuntas a few kms further on. During the dry season it is possible to drive down the stream bed until you come to a small man made concrete dam. At this point you pretty well have to stop as the ramp going down on river right is somewhat decrepit and pretty rough unless you have a high clearance vehicle. If you have a camper it is possible to camp just above the dam. A couple of hundred meters further downstream is the Balneario. It is possible to camp here with a small camper or a tent. Another option would be to take the main dirt road on to the village of Adjuntas, find your way through the town down to the stream bed, and then drive upstream to the Balneario. The Balneario is a good spot to use as a base for hiking in this area. After a hot day of hiking one can either bathe in the stream or hike over to the Balneario and use the pool for a small fee.

Route 8: Balneario El Oasis to El Canon del Paraiso

Time: 3 hours return
Distance: 7 km
Difficulty: Easy
Hazards: None
Elevation Change: Very little
Topo Map: F-14-C-57 San Pablo Tomilan
Attraction: Views of the river valley; small farms using irrigation

Starting from the front gate of the Balneario [N 20 59.855 ; W 99 42.573] and heading downstream, take the path that goes up and to the right past the Balneario. The path climbs for a short while, then drops back down to the stream. Walk along a small concrete aqueduct on river right. About 50 meters past the aqueduct look for a narrow dirt road heading off to the left from the stream bed. (Watch for overhead electrical wires crossing the stream at this point.) A bamboo fence runs along the road for a short distance. Follow this road (which climbs a bit and curves left) which leads to the valley of El Rio Extorax.

There is ample growth of bamboo as well as many small cultivated fields along the way using irrigation from the river.

After walking about 45-50 minutes, the road leads to a swinging bridge [N 21 00.779'; W 99 42.458']. Cross the bridge, then immediately turn left. The trail continues on past some houses with a fence running

Maureen crossing swinging bridge

along the left-hand side of the trail. In a few hundred meters the trail then drops down to cross the stream [N 21 01.007' ; W 99 42.125']. This usually only involves stepping from stone to stone. A few hundred meters further on you come to El Canon Paraiso across which a dam has just recently been built. It used to be that you could walk into this canyon for a kilometer or two, but now it's impossible to carry on any further on foot. The water being held back by the dam is now being used for irrigation and drinking.

Route 9: Canyon Extorax

Time: 3 - 4 hours return (depending on how far you want to go)
Distance: 6+ kms return
Difficulty: Moderate
Hazards: Some loose rock on trail in places. Otherwise good walking
Elevation Change: 200 meters
Topo Map: F-14-C-57 San Pablo Toliman; Also, F-14-C-47 and F-14-C-58
Attraction: Canyon views; small farms using irrigation

To reach the trailhead for this walk, there are three options: walk, cycle or drive. From the balneario (spa), head downstream again about 0.7 km. until you come to the junction of El Rio Extorax. At this point you will have the village of Adjuntas on river right. Walk/Cycle through the village and take the only dirt road that heads south-east along the right-hand side of the river. About 3 km down this road you will come to another small village located at the junction of El Arroyo Orduna and El Rio Extorax. El Arroyo Orduna flows in from the south and joins El Rio Extorax at this point. Here you will find a small tienda which sells soft drinks, beer and basic staples for the community. If you have bicycles it is possible to negotiate with the owner to look after them while you are hiking, or to keep an eye on your vehicle if you drive in. Usually patronizing the store is payment enough. I found the people very friendly here.

From the balneario, to drive to this trailhead you will have to go back the way you came in. Drive back up to the other dirt road that you initially came in on and turn left. This is a tight turn. If you feel you can't make it, turn right and go down the road about 1 km to find a wider place to turn around. This road switchbacks up and over a low mountain and comes back down the other side to the village of Adjuntas. This is a spectacular drive. It would also make an interesting cycle with a lot of puffing involved as the elevation gain is quite significant. You then have to drive through the village and out the other side to continue on the road south along El Rio Extorax. When you reach the tienda, you can park your vehicle here. It's a good idea to advise the people in the store. They may suggest where you can park without interfering with local traffic as space is at a premium. Before driving in, it's advisable to ask the locals in Adjuntas about the condition of the road as washouts or slides may have made the road impassable for vehicles. The road is fairly narrow, often only a single lane. If you meet oncoming traffic, you may have to reverse for some distance before finding a place to pass.

Starting from the tienda, cross the Arroyo Orduna and go up the other side past some houses. Once past the houses, the trail begins to drop down to the river bottom. Once at the river bottom the trail follows along river right through the canyon. Don't try to follow along the river itself. Stay right, as close to the hill sides as you can, and look for a path that goes for a short distance along a small irrigation canal and some small farms. Once past the small farms, the trail climbs for a short while, then drops down again to the river. At this point you will be about 1.5 km into the walk. Here you will find two alternate trails. One crosses the river, follows the river on river left for about 0.5 km., then crosses the river again back to river right further downstream. This trail is rather vague in places and I don't recommend trying to follow it unless you like the challenge of finding trails. Take the other trail that continues on river right and begins to climb in a series of switchbacks. This becomes what I call the "upper trail". The trail gains about 100 meters in elevation to a

point from where you can get some superb views of the river canyon and the surrounding mountain scape [N 20 59.564' ; W 99 40.373']. From this high point the trail begins to drop and switch back down to the river floor. At the river bottom the upper trail joins the previously mentioned lower trail coming in from the left [N 20 59.660' ; W 99 40.352']. Make careful note of where these two trails join so you can find the upper trail again on the way back. Turn right and keep following the trial downstream. After a few hundred meters both the river and the trail take a turn to the right.

After the turn the trail climbs somewhat again on river right and overlooks more small farms along the river. It follows along the river for another kilometer or so and then gradually begins to drop into another river valley [N 20

The trail along Extorax Canyon

59.747' ; W 99 39.841']. The trail is quite clear and you can follow it for as long as you have time and daylight. Just remember to give yourself enough time to get back before nightfall. To return you must backtrack along the same trail as described above.

Route 10: Canyon Arroyo Orduna

Time: 4.5 hours return
Distance: 8 km return
Difficulty: Moderate
Hazards: Some loose rock, otherwise good walking
Elevation Change: 240 meters
Topo Map: F-14-C-57 San Pablo Toliman
Attraction: Canyon and mountain views

To reach the trailhead for this walk, follow the description given for Route 8 to get to the tienda. From the tienda, walk up the dirt road heading south along the Arroyo Orduna. The road crosses the stream [N 20 58.723' ; W 99 40.527]. Continue on up the road for another 10 minutes or so until you come to some houses (about 1.25 km from the tienda). You will note the entrance to the canyon off to the right.

Follow the stream bed into the entrance way to the canyon. For the first kilometer you basically hike up the stream bed following other people's footsteps. During the dry season there may be a little water in the stream but nothing significant. You will note small irrigation projects along the way along with some black plastic hose used to conduct water further downstream. After about 1 km the trail branches by a large tree [N 20 57.922' ; W 99 40.483'].

At this point you have two choices: a path that goes up to the right or a lower path that follows a man made water channel for a short distance, then becomes a part of the natural water course. The path up to the right is easier but the stream bed has interesting rock formations created by water erosion. An option is to hike up the stream bed and then return via the path or vice versa. Note however that the walk up (or down) the stream bed will be more difficult as it involves climbing up and over some large boulders.

In another kilometer or so the canyon

Along the Arroyo Ordund trail

opens up [N 20 57.716' ; W 99 40.477']. A little further on the settlement of Culebras comes into view [N 20 57.352' ; W99 40.313'] situated in a beautiful valley. After appreciating the views and finding a good lunch spot under a shade tree or by a large rock, one can return either via the trail on the left-hand side of the arroyo (heading downstream) which takes you back to the big tree, or by hiking down the stream bed.

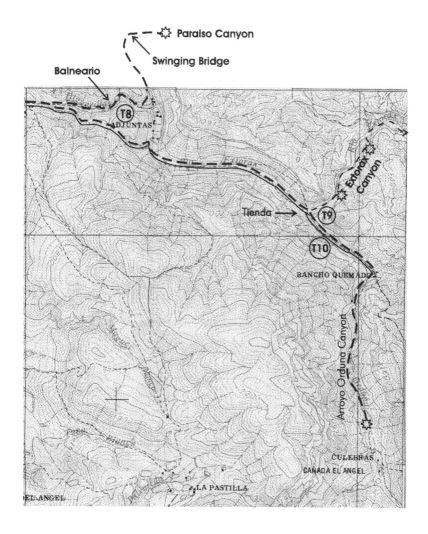

Route 11: El Parque Nacional Campo Alegre Campground to La Zona Arqueologica de Ranas.

Time: 5 - 6 hours
Distance: 9 km
Difficulty: Easy to moderate
Hazards: Occasional loose rock; otherwise good walking
Elevation Change: Very little up to the archeological zone
Topo Map: F-14-C -58 San Joaquin
Attraction: Archeological zone; valley views; small farms

Road Access: From the junction of highways Mex 4 and Mex 120 drive south on Mex 120 for approximately 10 km. Watch for highway signs directing you to San Joaquin. Turn left and follow the paved road east up into the hills to the town of San Joaquin. You have to drive right through the town and up the hill on the other side to get to the Campo Alegre Campground. As you enter the town watch for a small tourist office on the right-hand side of the street. The people here can help direct you towards the campground. Failing that, there is signage on the street directing you to the campground. Just follow the signs. This campground is a good base from which to do this hike and to explore the surrounding area.

Although one can drive from the campground [N 20 54.755' ; W 99 34.418'] to the archeological site, we recommend walking to the site in order to appreciate the wonderful views afforded by surrounding mountains and valleys. Facing east from the entrance to the campground you will see two streets branching away from each other. The one on the right heads down into the town. Take the street on the left that follows a high contour along the hill to the north side of town for about 0.75 km. This trail provides some magnificent views of the town. When you come to the next street junction, turn left following the archeological signs. This street takes you in a northerly direction out of town. It quickly turns into a dirt road which winds along the contours of the hills offering spectacular views of the surrounding countryside. Follow this road for about 2 + km to the archeological site [N 20 55.424' ; W 99 34.050']. This site is well worth a visit.

After spending an hour or so at the site, back track down the road you walked in on for about 200 meters till you come to a dirt road that goes off to the right (north) [N 20 55.768' ; W99 34.139']. There is a small restaurant here called Casa Chilo where you can stop for a rest and a cool drink. Turn right here and follow the dirt road. This road drops quickly down into the valley and then back up to the small communities of Trinchera and Tierra Colorada. We can recommend walking along this trail for a kilometer or two just for the views. The more energetic types can go on farther. This trail drops about 200 meters within a kilometer before it starts to climb again to Tinchera. You will have to return by this trial to its junction with the road back to town at the restaurant Casa Chilo. Turn right at the restaurant and retrace your walk back to town and to the campground.

Note: During the cool season (December - January) this area can become quite cloudy, misty and cool.

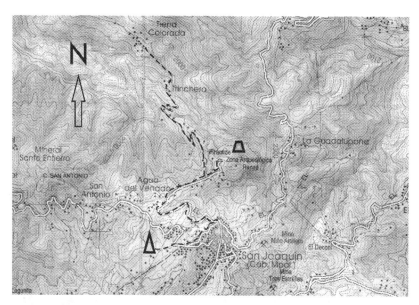

Route 12: Ruta Las Minas

Time: 4 hours return
Distance: 8 kilometers
Difficulty: Easy to Moderate
Hazards: Old mine shafts; high altitude
Elevation Change: 100+ meters
Topo Map: F-14-C-48 Jalpan
Attraction: Once out of the town area, this trail is uninhabited and a real pleasure to walk. It takes you through relatively untouched pine and oak forest. There are also a couple of good viewpoints along the way

Road Access: From the junction of Mex 4 and Mex 120, drive north for 52 km to the town of Penal de Amoles. This route takes you through some spectacular desert and mountain scenery.

The description for this walk will begin from the church located in the main plaza (town square). From the front of the church facing north, go past the Carneceria Camancho. Then walk across the main highway that runs through the town and walk up the street that goes by a "Fonda La Guerra Cervesa Superior" sign located at No.7 Calle Hospital (on the right-hand side as you go up the street). About half way up the street you pass the hospital on the right-hand side. It has the initials IMSS. After a few hundred meters the pavement turns into a dirt track which leads to some houses on top of the hill. After passing by these houses the trail begins to drop and follow along side the valley on the right. At this point there is a barbed wire fence running along the trail on the right-hand side and a rock wall on the left-hand side of the trail. Looking across the valley you can see the highway on the other side [N 21 08.502' ; W 99 37.591']. Some of the fence posts are made of wood and some of concrete. Some of the concrete ones are painted a reddish orange and white at the bottom. After a couple hundred more meters the track eventually narrows down to a single walking trail.

The track trail stops at a place where there has been a rock wall built up and filled in with soil on the right-hand side of the trail, probably in preparation for putting up a building. The fence line continues on and so does the rock fence. At about 1.5 km into the walk you will come to a fork in the trail. At this point a big tree stands in the middle which has been hacked at around the bottom [N 21 08.724' ; W 99 37.517']. Take the right fork which goes down and follows the fence line. It has been paved with flat rocks for about 200 meters. Eventually the barbed wire fence comes to an end. At this point you get a good view of a garbage dump [N 21 08.806' ; W 99 37.366']. The trail levels out for a while and then drops again. Here you will see a rock wall fence on the left-hand side running uphill [N 21 08.821' ; W 99 37.281'].

Once past the rock wall fence, the trail drops steadily as it follows the contour of the mountain. At one point you will come to a spot where the trail branches. You can take either trail as they join together again a short distance further on. Just a few meters past where the trails rejoin you will pass what appears to be an abandoned mine shaft going into the rock. You can still see how it was shored up with rock. About 20 meters beyond the mine shaft, you will come upon a concrete survey marker. In about another 20 meters or so you will pass a cleft in the rock on the left-hand side of the trail. This leads to another hole in the rock and was probably another primitive mine shaft [N 21 08.921'; W 99 37.280']. Past this point the trail levels out as it follows along the contour of a high ridge [N 21 08.948' ; W 99 37.268']. After a short while the trail climbs and heads in a northerly direction [N 21 09.094' ; W 099 37.270'].

At about 2.25 km into the walk you will come to a branch in the trail [N 21 09.182' ; W 99 37.240']. Take the right branch which will lead around a small ridge to another survey marker [N 21 09.392' ; W 99 37.127']. Along this path there is another hole going into the ground to the left of the trail. From the survey marker there are some nice views to the east. This is a good spot to stop for lunch. There is another hole in the ground near the survey marker which is probably another sign of the mining activity that took place here in the past.

After lunch, back track to the fork in the trail. Once back at the fork turn right and head north. Follow the trail till you come to a spot where there was a small excavation on the right-hand side. Part of a tree has broken off here and is suspended about 2 meters above the trail [N 21 09.457' ; W 99 37.209']. I recommend that you turn around here as the trail only proceeds on for another 100 meters or so, then becomes rather vague as it descends into the forest.

Walking along a forested section of the trail

Route 13: Aquaduct Trail.

Time: 4 - 5 hours
Distance: 8 km. return
Difficulty: Moderate
Hazards: Some loose rock; high altitude
Elevation Change:.240 meters
Topo Map: F-14-C-48 Jalpan
Attraction: Scenic views of the valleys sloping off to the south-east and south-west

Starting from the front of the church in the central plaza (with your back to the front entrance to the church), take the stairs leading down to your left to Avenida Independencia. Turn left on Ave. Independencia until you get to Calle Leona Vicario. Turn right on Leona Vicario and follow it to the primary and secondary schools on the right-hand side of the street. The secondary school is called "CECYTEQ Penal de Amoles". Just a few meters beyond the secondary school there is a concrete street that branches off to the left and goes up a hill with low buildings on both sides. Take this street. The concrete paving goes on for about 200 meters, then becomes a dirt track. The trail continues to climb gradually and leads up to some concrete tanks on the left-hand side of the trail. A 4 inch pipe comes out from one of the tanks and conducts water down to the town. At this point you have left the town and are well into the countryside.

Once past the water tanks the trail continues steadily upwards passing some houses along the way [N 21 07.860' ; W 99 36.637']. A little further on the trail tops out over a bit of a saddle between two hills [N 21 07.804' ; W 99 36.591']. Once over the saddle, the trail gradually begins to descend. About 2 km into the walk there is a little clearing on the right-hand side of the trail with a great view of the valley below [N 21 07.647'; W 99 36.380']. This is a good place to stop for a rest or have a lunch.

About another 0.5 km down the trail there is a small meadow offering more fine views [N 21 07.534' ; W 99 36.180']. The trail follows a fence line along the meadow for a short distance (about 100 meters) where the fence line ends. In about another 300 meters the trail comes along side a dirt road on the right [N 21 07.505' ; W 99 35.945']. The road turns to the right. The trail continues straight on past a concrete block building. It descends more rapidly now for about another 0.5 km where it crosses the road [N 21 07.389' ; W 99 35.765']. After crossing the road, it continues in a downward direction. We turned around here conscious of the fact that the more you go down the more one has to climb back up to return. However, more adventurous or ambitious folks may want to carry on for a while before returning.

Scenic Views from the trail

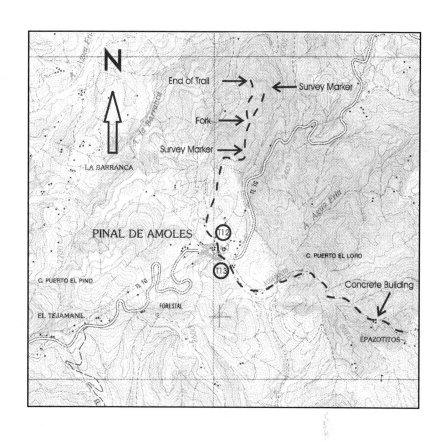

End of Trail →

← Survey Marker

Fork →

Survey Marker →

N

LA BARRANCA

PINAL DE AMOLES

C. PUERTO EL LORO

C. PUERTO EL PINO

Concrete Building

FORESTAL

EL TEJAMANIL

EPAZOTITOS

Oaxaca State

LOCATION OF THE STATE OF OAXACA AND TIME ZONES IN MEXICO

The two trails described in this state are located just outside the city of Oaxaca. Besides being a beautiful and interesting city to visit with its fascinating archeological sites, Oaxaca has two interesting trails to offer in San Filipe National Park located just on the northern edge of the city. The park is easily accessible by public transport. As bus schedules and routes may change, it pays to check with the city tourist office with regards to buses going to the park.

Oaxaca Trails Locator Map

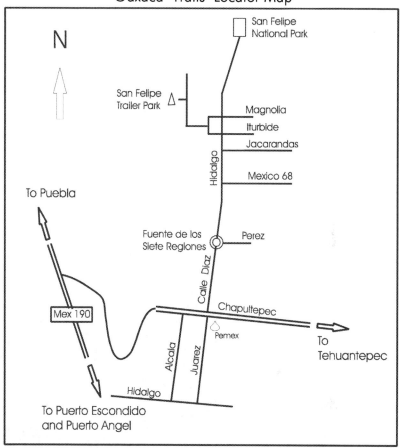

Accessing the National park from the Zocalo: Walk 4 blocks east on Ave. Hidalgo to Ave. Xicotencatl (which becomes Ave. Pino Suarez just a couple of blocks north). On Ave. Xicotencatl or Ave. Pino Suarez, catch the bus for the barrio of San Filipe. Take the bus to the end of the line. After getting off the bus and facing back the way you came, you will see a dirt road heading off to your right. Take this road and within a minute you will see the large entrance sign for San Filipe National Park. Within a ½ km you will come to a traffic control gate and a small shop selling cold drinks and water.

Accessing the park from the San Felipe Trailer Park: From the trailer park entrance gate, turn left and walk back to Calle Hidalgo. Catch the San Filipe bus here and take it to the end of the line. Then follow the directions as given above under "Accessing the park from the Zocalo".

Route 14: Las Cascadas.

Time: 7 hours
Distance: 8 km return
Difficulty: Moderate for most of the trail with short strenuous sections. Last 1km is strenuous
Hazards: Some loose rock near the end of the trail; high altitude
Elevation Change: 560 meters
Topo Map: E-14-D-47 Oaxaca De Juarez
Attractions: Scenic waterfalls; views of the Oaxaca valley; bring a bathing suit

This trail is quite popular with the locals, especially on weekends. With the snack shop to your back, the trail begins directly ahead of you, to the right of the bridge. Don't follow what looks like a paved road going off to the right. Within ½ km you will come upon a restaurant and a kiddie play area [N 17 07.174' ; W 96 42.617']. This place is open only on weekends and holidays. In about ½ km from the restaurant the trail passes a rock dam and a water storage area [N 17 07.426' ; W 96 42.417']. Within another 200 meters you will come to the first falls [N 17 07 526' ; W 96 42.200']. Continue on for another 200 meters or so and you will come to the second falls [N17 07.657' ; W 96 42.127']. Continuing up the path for about another 300 meters one comes to the third falls [N 17 07.818' ; W 96 42.003']. It is a bit of a climb to reach the top of this falls. Within a short distance beyond the third falls there is a branch in the trail [N 17 07.849' ; W 96 41.996']. Follow the right branch going upstream. Going on for about 3/4 km you come to the fourth falls which has a significant drop. This is a good place to stop for lunch and just appreciate the surroundings. At this point you have the choice of returning by the same route as you came in on or continuing on for about another kilometer.

This part of the trail is for the more ambitious types but it does reward you with some magnificent views of the Oaxaca Valley. A good pair of hiking boots is recommended for this portion of the trail. To continue on, the trail starts just to the right of the falls. It now becomes a steep climb over rock until you come out at the top of the falls [N 17 08.203' ; W 96 41.739']. Going past this point, the trail continues upwards. It becomes a steep climb and a real scramble over some loose rock for about 50 meters. Once past this, the trail levels out a bit and offers some great views of the valley. A little further

One of many waterfalls along the trail

on there is a fifth falls, but smaller than the others. It's a good place to stop for a refreshing dip after the hard climb. The trail continues upwards to the left of the falls. About 50 meters beyond the small falls is another viewpoint offering a great view of the valley [N 17 08.346' ; W 96 41.636'].

Although the trail does continue on, we recommend that you turn around here. Going on could be dangerous, especially when descending the trail on your return as it is quite steep with not much to hold on to. Should you slip and go out of control, you could wind up taking a long slide down the side of the mountain and getting seriously injured.

Route 15: Pena de San Filipe

Time: 7 - 8 hours return (depending on how far you go)
Distance: 17 km return
Difficulty: Moderate
Hazards: High Altitude
Elevation Change: 960 meters
Topo Map: E-14-D-47 Oaxaca De Juarz.
Attractions: Hike through oak and pine forests; scenic views

With your back to the shop, walk over to the bridge on your left. Once at the bridge, take the stairs that go down to your left and under the bridge. Once under the bridge, walk up the dry stream bed and cross over to the left side. Follow the trail up the left side of the stream bed. It heads up sharply to the left over a rocky surface. About 300 meters up from the bridge, the trail levels out for a short time with a pleasant walk through some eucalyptus trees [N 17 06.992' ; W 96 42.603']. The trail climbs gently and shortly enters a stunted oak forest. At this point there will be a 4 inch water pipe running along the trail [N 17 07.316' ; W 96 42.408]. The trail then drops down and crosses a stream. After crossing the stream you will see a trail branching to the right which follows the stream for a while [N 17 07.472' ; W 96 42.422'].

Continue on the main trail on your left. The trail now climbs steadily and is badly eroded. Within about 15 - 20 minutes you will come to another trail junction [N 17 07.517' ; W 96 42.378']. You will see what looks like several eroded trails coming in from your left. Turn left here and follow one of these trails. They quickly converge into one trail heading in an ENE direction. The trail is eroded and heads steadily upwards. After a short distance of steady climbing the trial enters a bluff of pine trees [N 17 07.689' ; W 96 42.377']. The trail now levels out for a while, then begins to climb again [N 17 08.049'; W 96 42.372'].

Occasionally along the trail you will notice a green arrow painted on a rock pointing up the trail. In about another 0.5 km you will find yourself walking high above a ravine on your left with water flowing below [N 17 08.259' ; W 96 42.305']. Within a couple of minutes you come to a fork in the trail. Continue on the trail that forks to the right. The left fork drops down into the ravine and up the other side. Once past the fork the trail climbs steadily and is in good condition. In about another 0.5 km the trail crosses a small open meadow and continues on up through the trees directly opposite [N 17 08.499' ; W 96 41.982']. Within another 200 meters there is another small meadow [N 17 08.516' ; W 96 41.822']. In a minute the trail crosses a small stream. Within 50 meters from the stream the trail forks. Take either fork as these trails rejoin again in a 100 meters or so further up the trail. The trails rejoin and go up to the left [N 17 08.504' ; W 96 41.673']. There is a bit of an open meadow here with the remains of a small rock fire pit.

A few hundred meters further on there is a fork in the trail [N 17 08.545' ; W 96 41.660']. The right fork goes down into a ravine. The main trail forks to the left and continues climbing upwards. The trail now passes through a mix of pine and oak forest. About 400 meters past the last fork the trail forks again. Take the right fork which continues upwards. In about another 10 minutes the trail forks once more. Take the left fork. In about 5 minutes the trail comes to a small clearing in the woods with a couple of logs across the trail.

It appears that this place has been used as a campsite in the past. This is a good spot to rest and have lunch. From here the trail continues ever upwards. The trail offers some good views of Pena De San Filipe. The trail now skirts to the right of Pena De San Filipe and heads towards the high ridge directly ahead. We hiked up to GPS reading [N 17 09.007' ; W 96 41.161'] before turning around. The trail does continue on and although the ridge looks temptingly close at this point, it is still about a 250 meter climb in altitude and over 2 km in distance to get to the ridge. If you do attempt to reach the ridge, make sure that you have enough time to get back down to the park entrance before dark.

Well worn path along the San Filipe trail

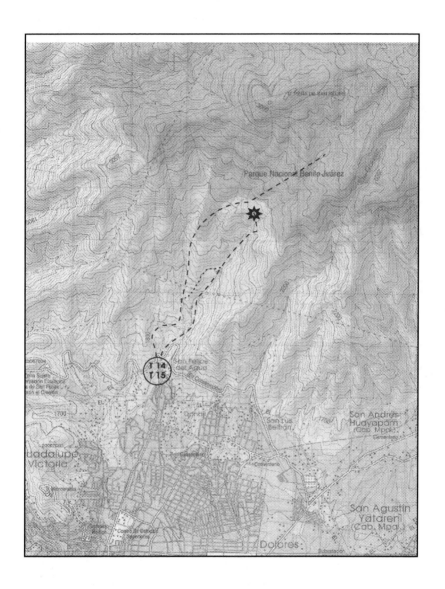

Mexico State

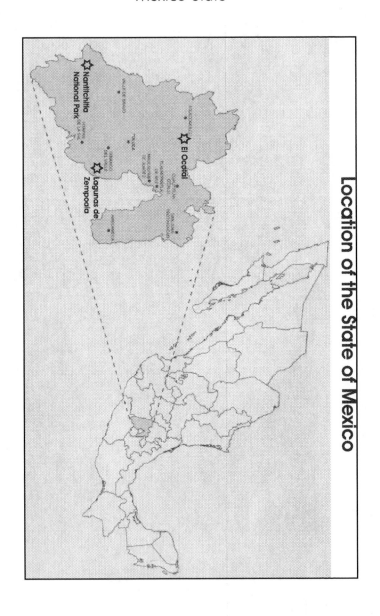

Location of the State of Mexico

Parque Recreativo El Ocotal Locator Map

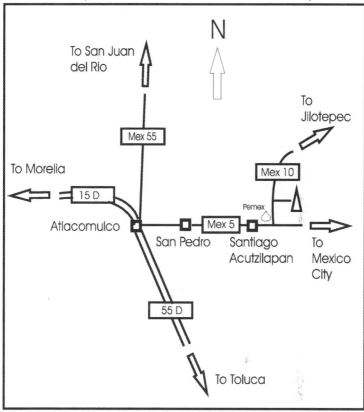

Route 16: Parque Recreativo El Ocotal to Cierro Dexini

Accessing the Area: About 70 km north of Toluca on Route 55D is the town of Atlacomulco. From Atlacomulco, drive east for about 13 km to the village of Santiago Acutzilapan. Just at the east end of the village there is a paved road heading north. Follow this road for about 2 km. The sign for the park is on the right hand side of the highway. El Parque Ocotal is a state park and campground with several hundred acres of pine trees and walking trails. It has a nice little hotel with a restaurant.

Time: 6.5 hours
Distance: 14 kilometers return
Difficulty: Easy to Moderate
Hazards: High altitude
Elevation Change: 430 meters
Topo Map: E-14-A-17 Atlacomulco
Attractions: Scenic countryside; great views at the end of the trail overlooking Isla De Las Aves

Starting from the hotel in the campground, follow the road north past the little lake and campsite No.7 [14Q 0421421; UTM 2190536]. The road turns left and follows the fence along the back part of the park. Follow the fence which runs in a NW direction to the sports grounds. Go out the gate and turn left on to the dirt road that runs behind the park along the fence line [14Q 0421283; UTM 2191028].

Follow the dirt road past the sports ground and the school to the junction with the paved road. Turn right and follow the paved road north for about 1 km. At this point [14Q 0421208; UTM 2191419] there is a dirt road that turns left off the paved road just before a retention pond on the east side of the paved road. Follow this dirt road straight ahead. A barbed wire fence with concrete posts follows the dirt road on the left-hand side. After about 200 meters the dirt road makes a 90 degree turn to the left (SW). Don't follow the dirt road, but continue straight on (WNW) following a dirt track past a couple of buildings and a rock fence on the right [14Q0421092; UTM2191548]. The dirt track passes some cultivated fields, then goes up hill and turns to the left. A foot path branches off from the dirt track and heads straight up [14Q 0420941; UTM 2191860]. There are some large boulders at this junction. Follow the foot path until it rejoins the dirt track coming from the left [14Q0420844; UTM 2191892]. There is a trail junction here. Take the dirt track that heads off to the right (north).

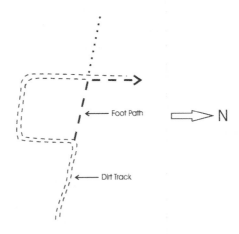

After a few hundred meters, there is a fork in the track [14Q 0420932; UTM 2192024]. Take the left fork. A little further on there are two more track junctions, both going off to the right [14Q0421127; UTM 2192423]. Don't take any of these diverging tracks but carry on straight ahead up and over a small rise. About ½ km further on there is another fork in the

View of Countryside from El Ocotal trail

track [14Q 0421267; UTM 2193049]. Take the branch going up to the right. At this point the trail is just on the edge of a continuous stand of oak trees. About 100 meters further, there is another junction. One track takes a turn to the right and begins dropping down. Don't take this track. Take the track that goes straight on and continues to climb.

This is a bulldozed trail, but it appears that only foot traffic uses it. Within another 50 meters there is a high barbed wire fence with green metal posts on the right-hand side. After another 200 meters the fence ends. Up to now the trail is in relatively open country, but from here on it is mostly treed. In about another 250 meters there is another fork in the trail [14Q 0421382; UTM 2193521]. Take the better used right fork. The trail now goes through a totally treed area. Another 300 meters further on, two lesser-used footpaths branch off to the right [14Q 0421502; UTM 2193813]. Continue

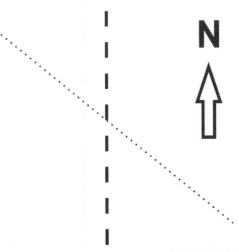

straight ahead on the main footpath. Within a ½ km, you will come upon what looks like a recently cut trail crossing the main trail at about a 45 degree angle [14Q 0421482; UTM 2194268].

Within another 500 meters the trail passes through a nice stand of pine [14Q 0421167; UTM 2194550]. Another 100 meters further the trail forks again. At this fork there is a large tree with the figure of a person carved into the trunk. Take the left fork. About 100 meters further, the trail passes through a small clearing among the pines and cedars. This makes for a shady lunch spot. About 150 meters further the trail passes through another small clearing among the oaks with a view through the trees to the south looking upon a valley and an extinct volcano [14Q 0420451; UTM 2194790]. 150 km further, there is another fork in the trail [14Q 0420224; UTM 2194923]. Here there is a good viewpoint looking down onto the flatlands and the town of Zaragoza. The right fork heads down into the valley. Take the left fork and continue to ascend. The trail goes on for another 600 meters or so until it comes out onto an open area and the highest point along the trail. From here there is a viewpoint overlooking a steep ravine and providing a beautiful view of the valleys to the south-west, west and north-west. The lake containing Isla De Las Aves can easily be seen to the south-west. To return, follow the same trail back to the state park.

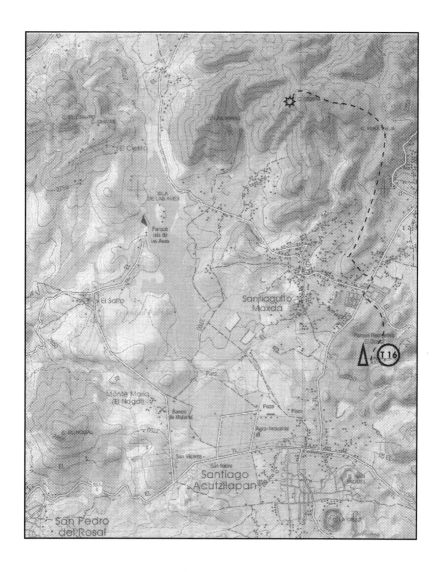

Route 17: Parque Cierra de Nanchititla

Accessing the Park: Take Mex 134 heading south-west from Toluca. Just past km 114 turn right onto Mex 2 for Luvianos. Go for 4.2 km on Mex 2 to the village of Estsanco. In the village there is a sign indicating the way to Nanchititla. Turn left at the sign. This road is mostly dirt all the way to Nanchititla and was being improved in places when we visited the area. It is about 35 km between Estanque and Parque Sierra de Nanchititla - mostly uphill. Because this road is somewhat rough, narrow and twisty as well as being a constant up hill grade, it will take from about 1.5 to 2 hours to reach the park - depending on road conditions.

Locator Map for Cierra de Nanchititla

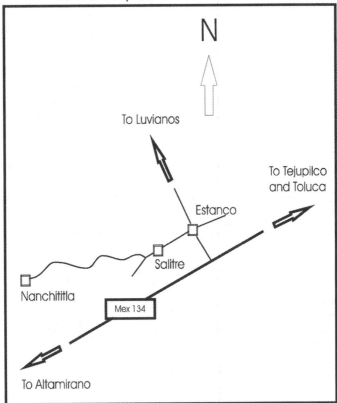

The park itself is very clean and well maintained. It is possible to camp or you can rent a cabin for a very reasonable fee. Since this park is an ecological reserve, it is necessary to take a guide with you into the park in order to hike the trails here. The guide is free - part of the service of the park.

Time: 5 to 6 hours depending how much time you spend at the falls
Distance: 6 km return
Difficulty: Easy to Moderate
Hazards: High altitude (1880 meters)
Elevation Change: 180 meters
Topo Map: E-14-A-55 Bejucos
GPS Location of Camp Site: 14Q 0349680; UTM 2085913
Attractions: An ecological reserve; great views of the falls and the valleys below; a variety of wildlife inhabits the area including deer and cougar

No trail map is provided for this walk as it is required to take a guide along on any of the trials that you intend to walk in this park.

A must see is the hike to the falls (Cascada de Nanchititla). Even in the dry season this can be a spectacular sight. Allow 5 to 6 hours for this walk. You'll want to take plenty of time to enjoy the magnificent views of the falls and the surrounding dramatic scenery. Other walks in the park can be arranged with the park administration. The name of the park administrator is Domingo Arce Pedraza. Telephone: 7222249675. The park staff are very friendly and accommodating. It is well worth spending a few days here to appreciate the wonderful scenery as well as the flora and fauna of the area. Some of the typical trees found here are pines, encinos and ocotes as well as many flowering plants. White tailed deer (venado) as well as mountain lion (puma) are found here.

Other than a small tienda in the village, there are no food services here. So it is wise to stock up on food in one of the larger towns along the way before coming. This is one of our favorite parks in Mexico partly due to the fact that it is obvious that great care and devotion are being put into its maintenance and protection.

Bungalow for rent in a well maintained park setting

Route 18: Lagunas de Zempoala Circuit

Time: 9 hours
Distance: 12 kilometers.
Difficulty: Moderate to strenuous
Hazards: Two steep ascents and descents; high altitude
Elevation Change: 850 meters
Topo Maps: E-14-A-49 Milpa Alta; E-14-A-48 Tenango de Arista
Attractions: Walk through forested area; scenic views; bird watching

Finding this hiking area takes a little perseverance as there are several towns and intersecting roads to navigate before getting here. Just to confuse things, route numbers on the road maps don't necessarily correspond with the route numbers on the highways.

Lagunas de Zempoala Circuit Locator Map

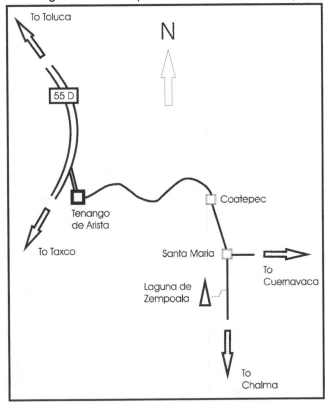

Access to the trail is found to the left of the children's playground located at the back end of the picnic site just behind the food stands [14Q 0466525; UTM 2106217]. Cross the bridge over the stream and start heading east following a good walking and horse riding trail. The stream will be on your right. Within a few minutes you pass through a gate. In another minute or so there is a fork in the trail. On the left fork there is a sign leaning on some bushes that says "Cabanas Indios" pointing to the left. Go straight ahead on the right fork staying on the main trail. In about 700 meters from the beginning of the walk the trail forks [14Q 0465901; UTM 2106016]. Take the right fork which crosses the stream.

Now keeping the stream on your left, the trail ascends into a forest of tall pines and groves of short cedars. The trail is wide and well-beaten. There is the occasional orange metal directional arrow nailed to a tree or splashes of orange paint sprayed on trees or rocks to mark the way. Sometimes there are deep blazes cut into tree trunks. About 40 minutes into the walk you cross the stream again. A short steep climb begins over tree stumps and rocks. Shortly there is another fork in the trail. An orange metal directional arrow indicates that you take the left fork. Actually, you can take either fork. They rejoin again in about 50 meters. A black arrow on a tree indicates the way. About 45 minutes into the walk a large deteriorating log bridges a small stream coming in from the right. Do not attempt to cross on the log as it is rotting and can be slippery. Follow the trail around to the right taking care as the rocks on the trail may be wet and slippery. Up to this point the trail is relatively easy. At the other end of the log bridge there is a fork in the trail. The left fork follows along the stream for a short while, then drops into the stream bed and continues on for a short distance. This is an interesting short side trip. With any amount of water flow this stream presents some beautiful cascades.

To continue the walk, return to the fork in the trail and take the right fork. There is orange flagging tape and a tin can nailed to a tree as well as a red arrow painted to a tree pointing down. Take the right fork. The trial initially climbs steeply, then for the next 25 minutes it becomes more moderate with some short climbs. About 1 hour and 45 minutes into the walk the trail becomes difficult. For the next 20 minutes the trail is steep with some loose rock underfoot and the odd log to crawl over. After this it becomes less strenuous and passes around some rock outcrops. About 2 hours and 10 minutes into the walk, the trail forks. Take the left fork. There was red tape across the right fork to keep people from going that way. GPS reading [14Q 0463750; UTM 2105390] is located about 400 meters up the trail from the last fork. The trail is easy to follow as it skirts along the mountain in a southerly direction. About 150 meters past GPS reading [14Q 0463739; UTM 2105190] the trail forks again. There is a large orange arrow on a tree pointing back the way you came. The main trail goes straight on (left fork) and was marked with orange flagging tape.

At this point you have the option of taking the right fork and hiking up to the rocky outcrops which you can see at the top of the mountain on your right. This trail becomes vague in places and requires some trail finding skills to get to the top. The climb up will take about 1 hour. Take note of any significant landmarks on the way up. Its easier finding your way up as you can see your destination most of the time. It's more difficult to return as you are now descending through pine forest and you can't see your destination. Noting landmarks or leaving markers along the route is useful in finding your way back. This is where flagging tape comes in handy. However, once on top you can spend some time rambling around and enjoying the views.

Once back at the fork in the trail, turn right and continue up the trail heading in a southerly direction. Within a kilometer the trail passes by a small shrine in the trees [14Q 0464160; UTM 2104482]. The trail goes off to the left of the shrine in a south-easterly direction. Within 500 meters the trail comes out to another shrine and a viewpoint [14Q 0464280; UTM 2104300]. The site is somewhat messed up with garbage and there is evidence of people having had fires. The trail forks here once more. Take the left fork. The trail descends into the trees in a north-easterly direction, then heads in an easterly direction with a bit of up and down. This branch of the trail is not as well used.

Within 1.5 km there is another viewpoint [14Q 0465695; UTM 2105090] affording a beautiful view of the valley to the south. Just a couple of minutes down the trail from the viewpoint there is another fork in the trail. There is an aluminum sign nailed to a tree that says "Chalma" pointing back up the tail. Take the left fork and continue descending. Within a few minutes there is another aluminum sign in the shape of an arrow (blue with yellow lettering) that says "Chalma". A faint trail forks to the right - ignore it. Continue descending to your left. The trail appears more well-used now. About 10 minutes further on, there is another fork in the trail. The left fork goes down the side of the mountain quite steeply. Take this left fork, descending carefully. You might have to grab onto the odd tree to control your descent. Within 300 m the trail descends past a rocky outcrop which affords some interesting views [14Q 0465950; UTM 2105886].

The trail continues to descend rapidly until it comes out to a small

View of ridges and valleys fron Cerro Zempoala

64

grove of small pines and cedar [14Q 0465967; UTM 2106020]. Walk down through this grove heading for the trail you started out on in the morning. The campground is visible to the right. Keep right and walk over a wooden bridge which crosses a stream and gully. Next you'll pass by a couple of decaying buildings. Walk past these buildings following the path which quickly rejoins the beginning of the trail. There is a red metal arrow nailed to a tree pointing back to the campground. Turn right here to return to the campground.

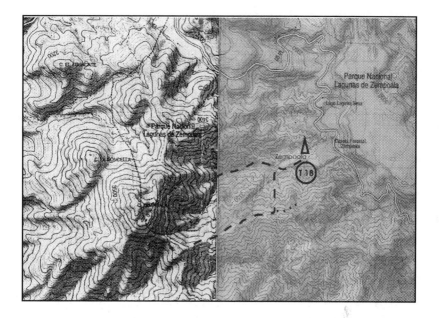

Michoacan State

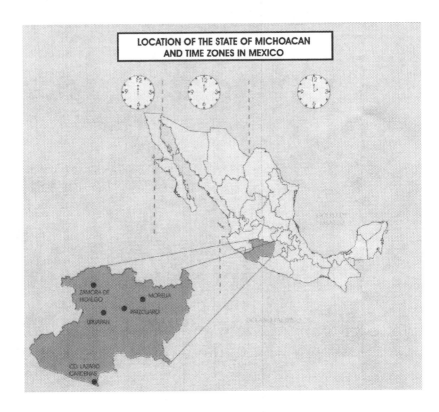

LOCATION OF THE STATE OF MICHOACAN AND TIME ZONES IN MEXICO

The two trails described here are located in opposite directions from Morelia. Route 19 is located west of Morelia via Patzcuaro and Uruapan. Route 20 is found east of Morelia via a beautiful mountainous drive along highway Mex 15 .

Route 19: El Centro Turistico Angahuan to Volcan Paricutin

Accessing the area: From the city of Uruapan, drive north on Mex 37 for about 12 km untill you come to a T-junction with a paved road coming in from the west. Follow this road for about 15 km to the town of Angahuan. As soon as you enter the town you will be encountered by men on horseback wanting you to hire their horse and ride to the volcano. If you are inclined to want to hire a horse, there is no need to hire one at this point. When you get to the park, there are plenty of people around wanting to rent you a horse for the day. To get to the park (called El Centro Turistico Angahuan) you have to drive through the town. The park has camping, cabins for rent and a restaurant with a great view of the volcano and the lava fields.

Angahuan Locator Map

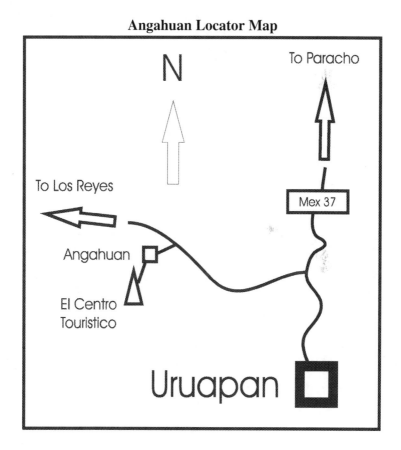

Time: 9 hours return
Distance: 20 Kilometers return
Difficulty: Moderate to strenuous at the end when ascending the volcano
Hazards: High altitude; loose volcanic sand in places along the trail making walking more difficult; loose rock on the final climb up to the top of the volcano
Elevation Change: 520 meters
Topo Maps: E-13-B-29 Paracho; E-13-B-39 Uruapan
Attractions: Views of the volcano and the lava fields: the remains of the temple of San Juan Parangaricutiro partly buried in the lava

For this hike, make sure that you get an early start and take plenty of water. From the tourist center [13Q 0790239; UTM 2162815], walk by the front of the restaurant and descend to the dirt track which passes just below the restaurant. Upon reaching the dirt track, turn left and head down past the tienda and a privately run restaurant where you can rent a horse if you wish. At the second restaurant the trail turns to the right and descends towards the old ruined church in the lava field. In about 700 meters from the park there is a fork in the trail [13Q 0789574; UTM 2162501]. Take the left fork. Within 300 meters from here there is another fork in the trail [13Q 0789284; UTM 2162376]. Take the left fork again. In another 250 meters the trail reaches the edge of the lava bed [13Q 0789034; UTM 2162314]. In the next 300 meters the trail passes through the lava bed and comes to a dirt parking area with stalls set up by the locals selling drinks and touristy things [13Q 0788735; UTM 2161978].

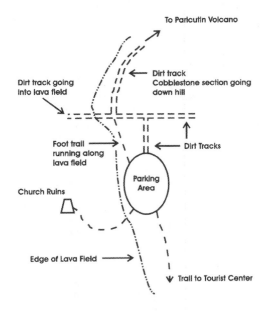

This area is accessible by vehicles using dirt tracks in order to visit the lava field and the remains of the church. The stalls are located on the left side of the parking area. When you get to the stalls, turn left, walk through the stalls and follow the trail over the lava to the church ruins.

Church ruins buried in lava

Once back at the stalls, skirt along the left side of the parking area. You will see a dirt track directly ahead of you. Just before the dirt track and to the left of it is a foot trail running west along the lava bed for a short distance. Take the foot trail. The foot trail comes out to a T-junction of two dirt tracks. Follow the dirt track directly ahead of you in a westerly direction. Within a very short walk from the T-intersection the dirt track has a cobbled stone section going downhill. This should confirm that you are on the correct dirt track heading towards the volcano. Once past the cobbled stone section the dirt track is topped with reddish colored cinders for a short distance [13Q 0788182; UTM 2162131]. This will put you just over 500 meters from the church ruins parking area.

About 1 km from the church ruins parking area the trail crosses over a small stone bridge and immediately comes to another T-junction [13Q 0787789; UTM 2162448]. Turn left at the T-junction. From this point on the walk to the volcano becomes more difficult due to this loose volcanic sand on the surface of the trail. You wind up using more energy and your pace slows down. Within a kilometer there is a fork in the dirt track [13Q 0786936; UTM 2162412]. Take the left fork. There is a little drink stand here where you can buy warm drinks. In another 800 meters the dirt track forks again. Take the left fork. Follow this dirt track for about 500 meters until you come to where the dirt track bottoms out at a water course and makes a sharp left turn at a large double metal gate. There is a small white

69

concrete marker just across the dirt track opposite the gate. The dirt track now heads in a southerly direction towards the volcano skirting the lava bed on the left.

Within a kilometer the dirt track passes through a barbed wire gate with stonework on either side. Continue straight ahead following the tire tracks and horse tracks, keeping the lava field on your left. About 1 km from the barbed wire gate the dirt track passes by a large tree on the right-hand side [13Q 0786679; UTM 2159568]. The tree is conspicuous as it's the only large tree in the area. Most of the vegetation here is quite stunted. The big tree casts a nice shade and is a good place for a rest stop. About 200 meters further on the dirt track ends [13Q 078690; UTM 2159559]. From here the trail becomes a horse and foot trail. It is very well used and obvious.

Follow the horse trail as it heads towards the volcano, keeping the two extinct volcanoes to your right. The trail approaches the volcano from the north-west. Near the base of the volcano there is another larger tree which is used by the horse riders to tie up the horses. Once at the base of the volcano the trail goes off to the right and spirals around up to the summit. This part can be somewhat difficult at times as you're climbing over loose sand and rock material at a fairly steep angle; however the views from the top are well worth the effort. Return to the tourist center by the same trail as you came in on. On the way back you may get offers from the horse owners to rent a horse for the return trip. Depending on how you feel you might want to take them up on the offer.

In late January of 1943 the people living in and around the village of Paricutin began hearing rumbling noises. On January 20 a local farmer and his wife were working in their cornfield when the ground began to rise upward forming a cradk about 2 meters across. Steam, sparks and hot ash began to be emitted. The farmers fled in fear. Within 24 hours a volcano began to form. Within a week it had grown to a height of 100 meters and rained ash on to the village. On June 12 lava began advancing towards the village and people began evacuating. A few months later the larger village of San Juan Parangariculiro was evacuated. By August most of Paricutin and San Juan were covered in lava and ash. Within a year the volcano had risin to a height of 410 meters above the surrounding land.

The volcano continued active until 1952. Today it is silent but on top and inside the cone there are still hot spots emitting sulfureous steam. Near the edge of the rugged lava field the remains of San Juan's two church towers stand in silent testimony to the powerful geological forces that altered the area.

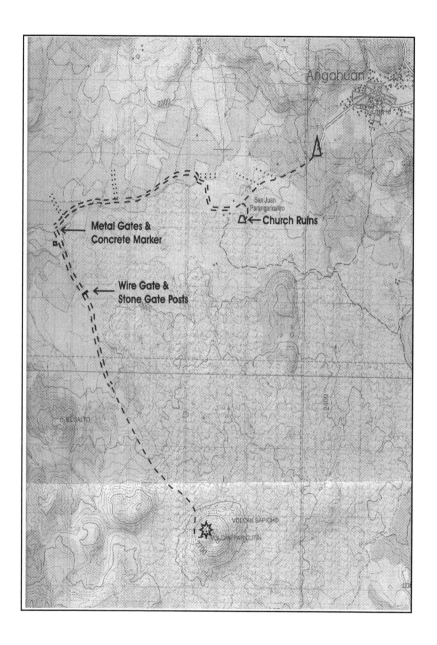

Angahuan

Metal Gates &
Concrete Marker ←

Wire Gate &
Stone Gate Posts ←

San Juan
Parangaricutiro
△← Church Ruins

Route 20: Presa Pucuato

Accessing the Area:: Presa Pucuato is situated in a mountainous area of pine forest. From Morelia take Mex 15 east to Mil Cumbres and Pucuato. This is a very beautiful drive through mountainous scenery. The road is very twisty but traffic is not too heavy. There is a scenic viewpoint at Mil Cumbres which is well worth a stop to view the mountainous landscape. The turnoff for Presa Pucuato is at km 156, just before the village of La Venta. The village of Pucuato (a separate village from Presa Pucuato) is signed off the highway. Turn off here and head south for about 9 km. At this point there is a little village just off to the right. This is the village of Presa Pucuato. Look for a sign that says "Restaurant El Delfin". It directs you into the village. You have to drive down through the village, cross a bridge below a dam, then up again to the other side. You then drive along the west shore of the presa for about 1.5 km until you come to a gate. Up to this point you can camp anywhere along the shore of the presa. This is a favorite spot for people to come in the evenings and weekends to do a little fishing. A short distance up from the gate there is an abandoned building and recreation area built on a rise overlooking the presa.

Presa Pucuato Trail Locator Map

Time: 7 hours
Distance: 18 km
Difficulty: Easy to moderate
Hazards: Domestic animals; high altitude
Elevation Change: 200 meters with some up and down
Topo Map: E-14-A-24 Tzitzio, Michoacan; Scale 1:50,000
Attractions: Open meadows and hills; views; good upland birding opportunities; camping is free

Start by going south through the first barbed wire gate [14Q 0323430; UTM 2169567] following the track trail to the abandoned recreation area (campamento). Walk ahead another 50 meters, then turn left and go through another gate. You are now off the track trail and on to a foot path. Follow the foot path for about 25 meters and go through a wooden gate. Continue on the path up the hill. A little further up there is a fork in the trail [14Q 0323432; UTM 2169137]. Don't take the left fork - keep going straight up the hill until you come to a fence line and another gate[14Q 0323482; UTM 2168912]. Pass through the gate and take the right fork immediately past the gate. The trail now drops down to an arm of the presa. Along the way you will notice sap collecting devices attached to the trees along the trail. The trail then passes through another fence, then across a drain coming down from the left. You will notice quite a bit of cattle activity here. After crossing this small pasture there is another fork in the trail [14Q 0323560; UTM 2168300]. Take the right fork with a wooden bridge crossing over a stream and go through a wooden gate. After passing through the gate, take the trail on the left which follows along the stream for about 50 meters and then begins to climb into the pines in a south-easterly direction. Within another 50 meters or so the trail emerges into a field with a fence line on your left. Follow the trail keeping the fence line on your left.

Within a few minutes you will come to a gate on your left which passes through the fence. Pass through the gate and continue following the trail now heading in a southerly direction through open, hilly pasture land offering some nice views of the surrounding hills. In 5 minutes the trail comes to another fence line and turns west following it. Within a few minutes the trail passes through another wooden gate [14Q 0322960; UTM 2167519]. At this point there is an inhabited building to the left of the trail. Once through the gate, continue on the trail heading west. Within 5 minutes the trail passes through a barbed wire gate. Just past the gate the trial forks. Take the right fork. Walk on for another 10 minutes or so till you come to where the trail passes through another fence line on your right and into the pines [14Q 0322125; UTM 2167110].

This is now a two track trail with fences on both sides of the trail. Within a minute the fences turn off to the left and the right. The trail continues on straight ahead heading west. Within a few minutes there is a footpath heading off to the right [14Q 0321898; UTM 2167135]. In another 15 meters there is another footpath heading off to the left. Stay on the main two track trail. Within 150 meters the trail intersects with another two track trail coming in from the right. Bear left. Within 15 meters there is another intersection with three trails. Take the right branch. Almost immediately the trail intersects with a well-used dirt road. Turn left heading down the road with a fence line on the left. Within 10 minutes the road joins with another coming in from the left. Bear right following the fence line on the left.

Within a few minutes the trail comes out to a well used road from the village of Pucuato. Bear left and walk along the road for a couple of minutes, then turn right on to a trail with piles of sawdust and some garbage. The trail forks immediately. Take the right fork heading down hill. The trail passes under electrical transmission lines. The village of Pucuato is visible just below and off to your right. In another 10 minutes the trail comes to a bridge over a stream [14Q 0320480;UTM 2166663]. Just before the bridge and on the left is a narrow footpath which follows between two fence lines to the left of the stream. Take the footpath heading west. Soon the trail turns south and begins climbing following along the left side of a stream. Within 15 minutes the trail comes to a recently made logging trail for trucks. Follow this for about 2 minutes keeping the stream on your right. The logging trail veers off to the left. Don't follow it, but rather turn right and cross the stream on a board that acts as a bridge. Immediately you'll pick up an old logging trail which is partly overgrown. Turn right and follow this trial downhill, keeping the stream on your right. Continue on until you come to where the stream on your right intersects with another stream coming in from the east. There are open fields and meadows on the right. The trail then follows along the stream and fence line on the right [14Q 0319870; UTM 2166524]. The trail continues on to the west through two fences with gates.

Eventually the trail intersects with a logging road running in an east-west direction and crosses the stream here [14Q 0319245; UTM 2166576]. Turn left and follow the logging road for about 1.5 km until you come to a junction in the road. The main road turns to the left. There will be a fence with a gate on the right [14Q 0318165; UTM 2165862]. Go through the gate. Immediately the road forks. Take the right fork. We went up the right fork for about 1 km before turning around at [14Q 0317615; UTM 2165892].

Note: To the west of the road that runs south of the village of Pucuato there is a lot of logging activity. Often foot trials are being turned into logging access roads for trucks. Things can change quickly. If the above description does not correspond with what you see, then it's advisable to turn around and return by the way you came.

Cattle along the trail

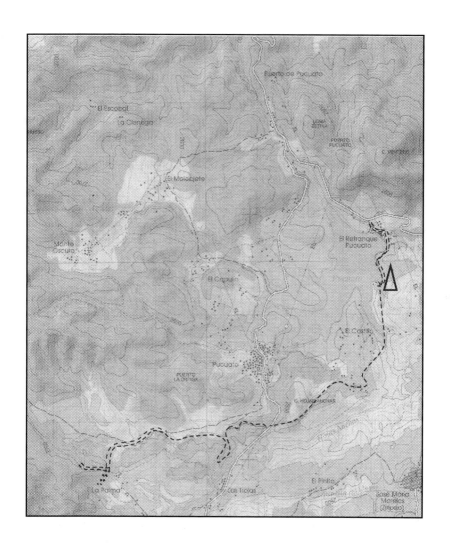

Guanajuato State

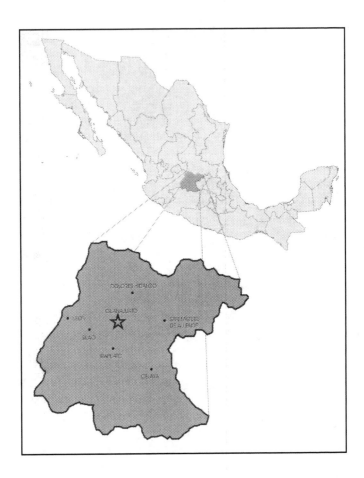

The next four trails (Routes 21 - 24) can all be accessed from the city of Guanajuato. This gives you the best of both worlds - the ability to stay in the city and enjoy its great restaurants and cultural life and still be able to do day hikes out into the surrounding hills. Guanajuato city also has a camp ground located on the northern side of the city which makes a great base for these hikes. Campground: Morrill Trailer Park. Phone: (473) 2-19-09. GPS Location: 14Q 0265928; UTM 2326344.

Guanajuato Trails Locator Map

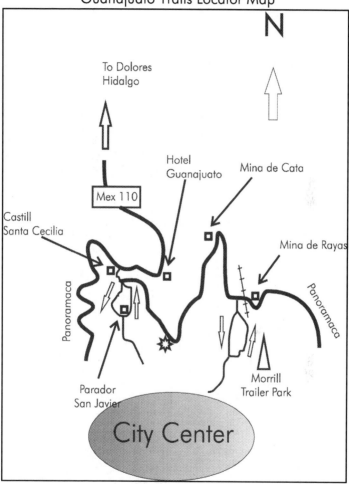

Accessing trails from the trailer park: Routes 21, 22, and 23 can be accessed on foot starting from the trailer park. All the others routes need to be accessed by car or bus.

Route 21: Los Santuarios Loop

Time: 7 hours return
Distance: 12 kilometers
Difficulty: Easy to Moderate
Hazards: High altitude
Elevation Change: 320 meters
Topo map: F-14-C-43 Guanajuato
Attractions: Scenic views; active mining operations; ruins of a church; two shrines overlooking the city

Once leaving the city, this trail takes you up and over rolling hills and open meadows offering some majestic views of the city nestled in the valley and the surrounding rugged landscape. Starting from the Morrill Trailer Park entrance, turn right and walk up the one way street to the Carreterra Panoramica (3 minutes). At the Carreterra Panoramica (C.P.), turn right and walk 50 meters to the stop sign at the railroad crossing. Then walk along the railway right-of-way past the Santa Fe mine complex gate and what looks like a castle behind it on your left till you come out onto the C.P again (10 minutes from the railway crossing). Turn right and walk along the C.P. past what appears to be the ruins of an old church and a small mining operation, both on the left hand side of the highway and about 5 minutes from when you came back out onto the C.P. Continue along the C.P. for another 5 minutes until you come to a mirador (a viewpoint with parking) overlooking the city [14Q 0266511; UTM 2326411].

Take the trail just behind the mirador that heads east up the hill and just to the left of three concrete electric utility poles. In a short while the trail comes to an electrical transmission line. Turn right and follow the trail which passes under the transmission line and then to the left of the lines [14Q 0266749; UTM 2326340]. After a few minutes the trail comes out onto a rise in the hill.

At this point the trail diverges to the left heading towards the mountain with a cross on top [14Q 0266818; UTM2326250]. The trail climbs steadily to the left traversing the contour of the mountain. Occasionally there is white paint on the rock to mark the trail [14Q 0267224; UTM 2326416]. About two-thirds of the way up the mountain there is a fork in the trail [14Q 0267486; UTM 2326424]. Take either fork. The right fork goes through a bluff of trees. The left fork skirts around the bluff. Both trails eventually re-join to becoming one again.

The trail now turns in a southerly direction heading for a saddle between two low hills [14Q 0267610; UTM 2326430]. Once achieving the saddle [14Q 0267658; UTM 2326322], you will see two white square markers about 150 meters off to the east. At this point turn right and start heading uphill in a westerly direction. Eventually you'll pick up a trail that leads up to the west, then switches and heads in a southerly direction [14Q 0267421; UTM 2326180]. You begin to get views of the presa in the valley to the east. As you head for the top of the mountain, the trail comes out onto rock. Now head for the highest point on which has been placed a white concrete cross overlooking the city. From here you get a beautiful 360 degree view [14Q 0267380; UTM 2326098].

Backtrack to the saddle. Once at the saddle, you will see a faint trail heading east over a low hill just to the left of the faded white square markers. Take this trail. In about 5 minutes there is a fork in the trail [14Q 0267855; UTM 2326390]. Take the left fork. Continue along for several minutes till you come to another fork. Note the white paint on the rock. Take the right fork. The trail continues until it comes to a rocky outcrop overlooking the presa below [14Q 0268343; UTM 2327000]. A little further on the trail crosses a wash [14Q 0268401; UTM 2327309]. In a little while there is another fork in the trial (more like a T-junction) [14Q 0268552; UTM 2327466].

One could turn left here to return to Guanajuato; however, we'll turn right and explore for a short while more. The trail drops off the hill, then bears left around the next hill with a valley to the left [14Q 0268725; UTM 2327642]. The trail continues along the top ridge overlooking the valley on the left [14Q 0268931; UTM 2327861]. This part of the trail has more trees. Although the trail does carry on, we walked up to GPS position [14Q 0269080; UTM 2327911], then turned around to return to the city.

Return to the T-junction. From here one can see the town of Santa Rosa off to the north north-east. From the T-junction go straight ahead to get on to the return loop to Guanajuato. Turning left will take you back onto the trail you came in on. After several minutes the trail crosses just above the wash [14Q 0268382; UTM 2327347]. You can see the other trail that you came in on just below crossing the wash. In a short while the trail takes a turn to the south [14Q 0268176; UTM 2327176]. After several more minutes, there is another fork in the trail [14Q 0268070; UTM 2326940]. Take the right fork. The trail now swings to the west and begins descending. As the trail descends west down along the ridge, one is able to get some great views overlooking the city [14Q 0267486; UTM 2326779].

Eventually the trail comes out onto the end of the ridge overlooking a shrine about 150 meters below [14Q 0267140; UTM 2326918].

Religious shrine found along the trail

Head for the shrine and then follow the trail down to the C.P. The trail is well marked with white paint on the rocks. The trail comes out at the C.P. Cross the C.P. and pick up the path that passes by the big rock and descends to the mining railway line. Follow the railway line back to the campground.

Route 22: Presa Pequena

Time: 6.5 hours return
Distance: 12 kilometers
Difficulty: Moderate
Hazards: High altitude
Elevation Change: 350 meters
Topo Map: F-14-C-43 Guanajuato
Attractions: Dams; birding; views of the hills, valleys and streams north of the city; swimming

From the Morrill Trailer Park entrance, turn right and walk up the one way street to the Carreterra Panoramica (3 minutes). At the Carreterra Panoramica (C.P.), turn right and walk 50 meters to the stop sign and the railway crossing. Once at the rail crossing turn left and take the street going uphill. The name of the street is Camino Real de las Minas. Within a few minutes you will come to an intersection with a U-turn sign and a one-way sign. Bear left onto Calle de la Cruz Pajaro. Within a minute or so you'll come to a fork in the street. You can take either fork. Both these streets re-join further up the hill. You'll see the big church ahead dominating the hill. When you reach the vicinity of the church, bear left and continue following the street past a small basketball court. After another minute or so the paved street ends and turns into a dirt road.

There is a large yellow building on the left. On your right is what appears to be a stone and concrete waterworks structure [14Q 0266345; UTM 2327133]. Here the dirt road forks. Take the right fork past the waterworks structure. Off to the left as you head down the dirt road you can see what appears to be a slurry pit from a mining operation. After about 10 minutes of walking from the waterworks building, you come to a fork in the trail [14Q 0266927; UTM 2327454]. You can take either trail as they re-join in a few minutes. If you take the right fork, you will notice two white square concrete markers on your left where the two trails re-join.

About 15 minutes down the road you'll come to a small fenced cattle enclosure with gates located right on the road [14Q 0267454; UTM 2327835]. If it is gated, you can walk around it on the right. A few meters past the cattle enclosure there is an entrance to a couple of mining tunnels. Just a few meters past this the road forks. Take the left fork. The road now follows the contour of the hill on the left. At one point it overlooks a small farm (finca) down below in the drainage to the right. Continue on up the road until you come to a fence line with a barbed wire gate [14Q 0268336; UTM 2328330]. This finca is located about 0.5 km north of the small cattle enclosure. There are some tall eucalyptus trees just off to the right.

At this point the dirt road stops and a foot trail carries on. Turn left at the barbed wire gate. The trail follows the fence line. Within a couple of minutes the trail passes by two iron rails stuck vertically into the ground. Within 200 meters there is another barbed wire fence with a gate [14Q0268555; UTM 2328504]. Just after the gate the trail passes a new adobe structure with a tin roof as well as some older adobe walls remaining to the right of the trail. In another 50 meters or so the trail passes by a small presa on the right [14Q0268658; UTM 2328550]. This is a good place to stop for lunch and maybe a swim. Good birding here - warblers, phainopelas and others. In another 100 meters up the trail there is an old rock wall dam across the stream [14Q 0268775; UTM 2328681]. It no longer retains water, but it's an interesting site to explore. There is a fork in the trail here. Take the right fork. Within a few minutes the trail drops down into the stream bed and then up to the left. A few meters after climbing out of the stream bed, you come to what appears to be another fork in the trail. Take either path. They re-join within a few meters.

After this, the trail begins to climb. Looking back, you can see Presa Pequena [14Q 0268895; UTM 2328742]. Here the trail is a little vague in places but shortly becomes distinct again. In another 100 meters the trail crosses the stream bed over exposed rock [14Q 0269104; UTM 2328818]. Bear right. The trail picks up again, climbing out of the watercourse, making a bit of a U-turn and heading in a southerly direction. Walk along a faint path for about 200 meters, then turn left (east) and walk up to the oak bluff on the ridge above you. There is no trail here, just open country walking. Upon entering the oak bluff, keep walking east till you get to the top of the ridge. You will come upon a foot path running along the ridge in a more or less north south direction. Turn left (north) and follow the path.

View of the dam and surrounding hills

In a short while (200 meters) you will come upon a good viewpoint with a large oak tree offering some welcoming shade [14Q 0269295; UTM 2328735]. This is a good place to take a break and enjoy the views. From here, the trail heads off in a northerly direction over an open gravel and rocky saddle area. The trail stays up along the ridge but may be a bit faint at times. There are a couple of white square markers off to the left. Once past the saddle, the trail begins to climb towards the ridge to the north-west [14Q 0269405; UTM 2329167]. It climbs gradually to another small gravel saddle, then turns south [14Q 0269363; UTM 2329255]. In about 100 meters the trail crosses through what appears to be a disused cart track, somewhat eroded and overgrown [14Q 0269280; UTM 2329166]. Shortly, the cart track turns into a faint trail heading down in a southerly direction. About 250 meters past the disused cart track, the trail passes over a gravel and rocky outcrop displaying yellow, orange and purple rock [14Q0269068; UTM 2328928]. From here Presa Pequena is visible. The trail now drops rapidly towards the presa. Follow it back to the presa. You are now on the same trail that you came in on. Take the trail back to the city.

Route 23: El Camino de Minas Viejas

Time: 3 to 4 hours
Distance: 6 km
Difficulty: Easy to Moderate
Hazards: High altitude
Elevation Change: 200 meters
Topo Map: F-14-C-43 Guanajuato
Attractions: Good birding along the stream; remains of past mining activities

From the Morrill Trailer Park entrance, turn right and walk up the one way street to the Carreterra Panoramica (3 minutes). At the Carreterra Panoramica (C.P.), turn right and walk 50 meters to the stop sign at the railway crossing. Turn right at the railway crossing and walk along the railway right-of-way past the Santa Fe mine complex gate and what looks like a castle behind it on your left till you come out onto the C.P. again (10 minutes from the railway crossing). Once at the C.P., cross it and go slightly over to your left. You will see a crumbling masonry rock wall on the other side of the highway. Go just to the left of it where you will pick up a footpath heading up and over a mound of broken rock dumped here from old mining activities. You'll see white paint splashed on some of the larger rocks as you go up.

From the top of the mound you will see three trails branching off: one to the right with white paint on the rocks leading to the shrine up on the hill overlooking the city and one to the left with white paint on the rocks and the concrete base for the security fence. Don't take either of these. Take the middle trail going straight ahead under the trees and then to your right along the security fence line. To your left there is a mining operation that is still active. Follow the trail along the fence line which shortly turns into a fence line with what looks like a moat. Here there is a lot of evidence of past mining activities.

Just ahead there is a metal gate and what looks like a disused security building and a security fence line for a short distance on the left [14Q 0266755; UTM 2326938]. The trail, which is actually an old mining road, is directly ahead. The trail climbs gradually but steadily upwards following along the contours of the large hill on the right. The stream and some little gardens can be seen down below. In about a kilometer there is a fork in the trail. The left fork heads down towards the stream. We'll be coming back to this point and taking this trail in a little while; however, for now, take the right fork and continue along the dirt track. At a point along the trail one can over look the stream with tall eucalyptus trees growing along its banks below [14Q 0267411; UTM 2327498]. Within a kilometer the trail comes to a fence. This is the end of the upper trail. Do not try to go beyond here as this is private property. Backtrack to the fork in the trail.

Once back at the fork, follow the trail heading down to the stream. Cross the stream and you'll come to another old abandoned trail running along the stream. From here, turn right and walk along the trail that follows the left side of the stream (heading upstream). Soon you will come to the stand of eucalyptus trees that could be seen from the upper trail. This is a good place to stop for a lunch under the shade of the eucalyptus. Just over along the east edge of the eucalyptus trees along the stream there are the remains of a rock foundation. Also, note how the trees are all growing in a row, evidence that people lived and worked in here in the past.

Lindi enjoying the view from the trail

Proceeding beyond the stand of eucalyptus trees, head upstream for another 10 minutes or so until you come to an old water control structure, now in ruins, built in 1901 out of rock and mortar. The date is still visible on the structure. Just beyond are more old structures built out of rock. One could spend an hour or two just exploring along this stream. Occasionally, you may have to share the trail with the local cattle that are allowed to roam the hills and valleys.

Go back to where the lower fork of the trail crossed the stream. Continue straight ahead and follow the trail on the right hand side of the stream heading downstream. Immediately on the right side of the trial you'll come upon a masonry stone entrance to an old mine shaft. Although it looks intriguing, it's probably not advisable to go venturing into the tunnel as one can never be sure just how safe these old mine tunnels are.

As you continue down the trail, you'll see more evidence of water control works and tile tubing to conduct water along the right side of the stream and hill. Shortly, the trail begins to climb up to the right and follows along the remains of an old road [14Q 0267115; UTM 2327420]. Further on the old road disappears but the trail continues to climb gradually but steadily. The city begins to come into veiw [14Q 0266954; UTM 2327325]. A little further on there is a fork in the trail [14Q 0266860; UTM 2327255]. Looking across the valley you can see the route you came up on. The trail now climbs through a grove of organ cactus and agave type plants.

Eventually, the trail tops out overlooking the Carreterra Panoramica [14Q0266653; UTM 2327182], then drops down through some interesting rock and turns to the right. The trail now heads in a westerly direction. Looking back, a couple of old mine tunnels can be seen going into the cliff face. In a few minutes the trail joins with a wider, more used trail [14Q 0266562; UTM 2327218]. This trail in turn junctures shortly with the return route from Presa Pequena (Route 22) [14Q 0266523; UTM 2327245]. Turn left and follow this road back to the city.

Upon coming to the white waterworks structure, you will see the beginning of the paved road on your left heading down past the large yellow building on the right. Walk down past the small basketball court on the left and proceed past the church on your left. Shortly you come to a fork in the streets. Take either fork. The left fork is shorter. Within a few minutes the streets re-join. Turn left. In a couple of minutes the streets fork again. Take the right fork and descend for another minute or two. There is another fork in the streets. Take the right fork and continue descending to the Carreterra Panoramica. You'll come out where the railway line crosses the C.P. Turn right here to return to the campground.

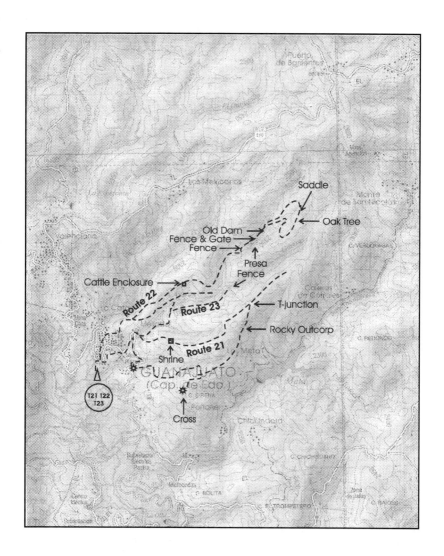

Saddle

Oak Tree

Old Dam
Fence & Gate
Fence

Presa
Fence

Cattle Enclosure

Route 22

Route 23

T-Junction

Rocky Outcorp

Route 21

Shrine

GUAMEDIATO
(Cap. de Edo.)

T21 T22
T23

Cross

Route 24: La Bufa

La Bufa Trails Locator Map

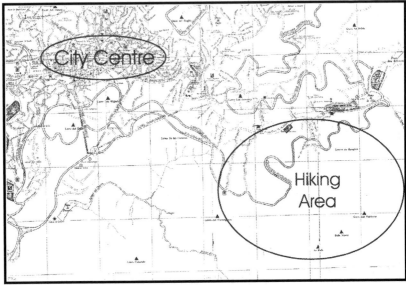

Time: 4 hours
Distance: 6 kilometers
Difficulty: Easy to Moderate
Hazards: High altitude
Elevation Change: 350 meters
Topo Maps: None
Attractions: Scenic views of the city; overhanging rock; religious shrine

No GPS coordinates will be given for this walk as the route is fairly easy to follow. The beginning of this walk is located in the east end of Guanajuato City. This walk starts from the corner of Paseo de la Presa de la Olla and Callejon San Juan de Dios. Walk up Callejon San Juan de Dios for a couple of minutes. The street swings to the left; however, take the stairs directly ahead which take you up to a short street. Turn right onto this street which almost immediately crosses the Carreterra Panoramica. Cross the Carreterra Pamoramaca and continue following this street for about 100 meters going uphill. This street then branches to the left and right (cobblestone to the left, paved to the right). Turn right and pass around a set of big metal gates. The paved street quickly turns to dirt and swings around to the left (south) going steadily uphill. Once going south you will see the peak of Bufa Nueva directly ahead. After another 100 meters this uncompleted street

86

swings to the left again heading somewhat easterly.

At this point keep going south (straight ahead) and pass under the two electrical transmission lines. In other words, keep going straight ahead and up towards Bufa Nueva. Go past the steel fence and continue climbing until you come to a dirt road. This road comes up from a parking area down to the right, just off the Carreterra Panoramica. Turn left and walk up the road until you come to a tree on the left-hand side with an arrow on it indicating a sharp right turn around a large boulder. The dirt road continues to ascend. Keep walking for another 5 minutes or so until the trail begins to swing around to the south again. Walk along for another few minutes until you come to where there are five white arrows pointing in various directions painted on some brown rock outcrop. You can begin the ascent here and approach La Bufa from the back side.

The road continues on and in a couple of minutes you'll come to some impressive overhanging rock with a small shrine built under the overhang (see picture). There is a lot of graffiti on the rock and the shrine. The trail goes on past the overhanging rock and the shrine (note the orange arrow) and under a large leaning rock. Just after the leaning rock there is a fork in the trail. A foot trail heading off to the left will take you up to the top.

If you take the right branch and continue on, you'll pass by a large work of graffiti with the word "Gretas" written in bright green capital letters. The trail now circles around the bottom of La Bufa from west to south, climbing steadily to bring you up to the top of La Bufa from the back side. The tops of La Bufa and Bufa Nueva offer some great views of the city nestled in the valley and also of the surrounding country. Once up here, you can ramble around enjoying the open country and the views.

From La Bufa you have the option of returning on the trail you came in on, or of following the trail that passes around the back side of Bufa Nueva and past Cerro Las Mantecas to complete a loop back to the city. After leaving

Overhanging rock and shrine

La Bufa, the trail intersects with the two trails mentioned earlier coming up from the trail below. Stay right and pass around the back of Bufa Nueva with the option of going to the top of it to get a different view of the surroundings. The trail around the back sides of La Bufa and Bufa Nueva may be a bit vague at times as it passes over bare rock, but if you keep a careful eye out, you will be able to see where the foot traffic has gone. Once past Bufa Nueva, the trail begins to descend and bend around to the left (north). Within a half kilometer there is a fork in the trail. Take the left fork and continue descending between the peaks of Bufa Nueva and Cerro Las Mantecas. The trail passes down below and in front of Cerro Las Mantecas and descends to a ridge. It then descends along the ridge heading for the Carreterra Panoramica, passes under two electrical transmission lines and over a low stone fence. Once on the Carreterra Panoramica, cross over to the street that runs past a green sign that says, "Palacio del Gobierno del Estado". Follow this cobble stone street back down to Paseo de la Presa de la Olla.

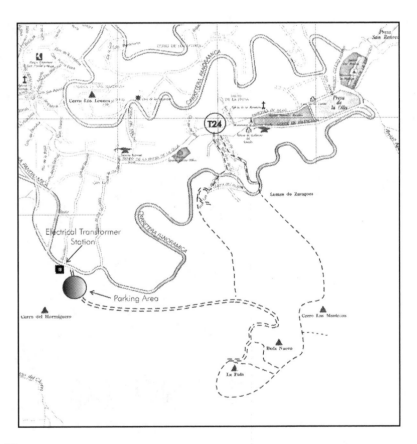

Routes 25,26,27 Locator Map

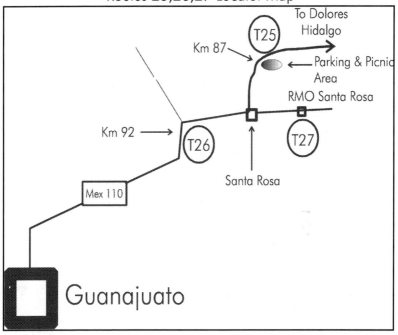

Route 25: Guardabosque Trail

Accessing Trail: Take Mex 110 which leaves from the north end of the city and runs northeast to the town of Santa Rosa de Lima and on to the city of Dolores Hidalgo. At km 87 (1.9 km past the town of Santa Rosa de Lima) is a parking area on the right-hand side of the highway with some concrete picnic tables. Across the highway there is a white sign that says, "Gobierno del Estado de Guanajuato" along with a security wall built of rock and mortar with coiled barbed wire on top. Needless to say this is private property. The trail is found to the left of this property and the barbed wire fence with green fence posts.

Time: 4 hours
Distance: 5 kilometers return
Difficulty: Easy to moderate
Hazards: High altitude
Elevation Change: 220 meters
Topo Map: F-14-C-43 Guanajuato
Attractions: Valley views and ridge rambling

This trail is quite a pleasant half-day jaunt. Note that the trail descends moderately but consistently. You will be coming back on this trail to return to the trailhead; therefore, be aware that the return trek will be mostly uphill but certainly not strenuous. Follow the barbed wire fence line and then the steel security fence on the left for about 75 meters. The trail then turns left and descends into a wash created by the stream coming down from the left. The trail follows this wash downstream. Within 5 minutes this trail intersects with a better used trail. Make note of this intersection as you will be returning by this route. Turn right here. Walk along for about 100 meters. There is a bit of a scramble trail that goes off and up to the right [14Q 0272530; UTM 2333166]. Don't take it. If you look back up the trail, you will see a house which has one entire side covered with windows. Whoever built the house picked a great location to take advantage of the views.

After more walking there is a fork in the trail [14Q 0272504; UTM 2333455]. Take the left fork which descends down the hill. Walk down about 50 meters. From here you will see three buildings below in the valley. The trail forks again. Take the left fork which shortly takes you out onto a ridge called Cerro Los Caballos overlooking a beautiful valley[14Q 0272416; UTM 2333596]. Looking back, you can still see the house with glass windows. Return to the last fork in the trail, turn left and contine on down the tail. The following are GPS points along the trail as you descend [14Q 0272680; UTM 23336000/ 14Q 0272630; UTM 2333735/ 14Q 0272818; UTM 2334042; 14Q 0272835; UTM

View of mountain ranges receding to the north

2334227]. About half way along these points, the trail branches once again. Take the left branch and continue descending. Follow the trail until you come to a yellow "X" painted on a rock. Turn left here and head south over the knoll. Looking back from here the fire tower (guardabosque) is visible. The knoll makes for a good lunch and rest spot offering great views of the valley and the range of low mountains to the north. You can spend time just rambling along the ridges here enjoying the views. This is the end of the trail. Return to the trail head by the same trail that you came in on.

Route 26: Mirador Superior Loop

Accessing the trail: Take Mex 110 which runs north from Guanajuato to Delores Hidalgo. Just past the km 92 road marker on the left-hand side of the highway there is a large blue and green sign with animals painted on it which says, "La Cuenca de la Esperanza". Just past the sign and around a sharp curve is the access road to the Fundacion Ecologia. Follow this cobblestone road for about 400 meters to the Fundacion and park your vehicle there.

Time: 3 to 4 hours depending how long you spend rambling in the hills
Distance: 4 km
Difficulty: Easy
Hazards: High altitude
Elevation Change: Very little
Topo Map: F-14-C-43 Guanajuato
Attractions: Great views of Santa Rosa and the surrounding hills and valleys; hill rambling

Walk back down the cobblestone road for about 150 meters till you come to a 3-way junction. Take the cobblestone road on your right (heading east) which quickly turns into a dirt road. In about 250 meters the road forks. A dirt track goes up to the left. There is a low square stone marker just to the left. Keep right and continue along this right fork. Go on another 50+ meters where you will pick up a foot path heading off to your right through an oak forest [14Q 0270271; UTM 2331070]. At this point it's worth a side trip down the road about 100 meters to your left to get a view of the town of Santa Rosa and the valley to the south. After taking in the views, return to footpath and follow it heading south. About 350 meters past the junction of the footpath with the dirt road, the trial forks [14Q 0270340; UTM 2330741]. Take the right fork. Within 400 meters from this fork the trail comes out onto some open hills and meadows. This is a good place to spend some time and just ramble. From the top of the first hill that you see ahead of you as you come out of the oak forest one can get views in all directions of the surrounding hills, meadows and valleys [14Q 0270284; UTM 2330372].

Just after coming onto the meadow from the oak forest, the trail bends to the right and heads in a westerly direction. Just below the first hill and on your right as you are facing south is an abandoned dirt track running in a north-south direction [14Q 0270202; UTM 2330478]. Turn right here and follow the dirt track as it heads in a north-westerly direction until it comes to some round stone markers and a junction with a road [14Q 0270032; UTM 2330605]. Turn right to return to the ecological center. One could turn left here to do more walking and then come back on the same road to the ecological center.

Open vistas of mountains

Route 27: Camino RMO Santa Rosa

Accessing the Trail: From Guanajuato take Mex 110 north to Santa Rosa de Lima. As you pass through the town of Santa Rosa de Lima, you'll come to a sign pointing to RMO Santa Rosa. Immediately after turning right off the highway you'll see the Restaurant La Sierra on your left. Pass the restaurant and keep left. The main street heads up hill through the town. The street turns into a cobblestone road and continues to climb. After 2 kilometers you reach the small village of RMO Santa Rosa. Just before driving into the village, on the left is a dirt road that goes up to the microwave towers. Almost opposite there is a dirt road that branches to the right heading south. Park your vehicle here [14Q 0272890; UTM 2331980].

Time: 3 hours
Distance: 5 kilometers return
Difficulty: Easy
Hazards: High altitude
Elevation Change: 50 meters
Topo Map: F-14-C-43 Guanajuato
Attractions: Pine forests; open meadows; views of surrounding countryside

RMO Santa Rosa Locator Map

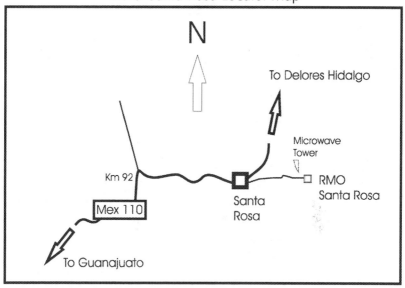

Follow the dirt road heading south. This is a rough dirt road really only suitable for 4X4's although you may see the occasional standard 2-wheel drive vehicle on it. The road travels along a high ridge. In about 500 meters the road comes to an open area [14Q 0272965; UTM 2331480]. 50 meters off to the right is a viewpoint overlooking the town of Santa Rosa and the valley to the south. About 250 meters further on there is a footpath that branches off to the right through the forest [14Q 0273040; UTM 2331237]. It's optional as to whether you take the path or continue on by the road.

The path is a little more interesting to walk. It eventually comes back out on to the road. The trail now passes over an expanse of open meadow which is used as an unofficial recreational area by the locals. About 1 km south of the above mentioned viewpoint the trail passes another viewpoint on the left overlooking a recently constructed water retention dam [14Q 0273464; UTM 2330266].

There are many rocky outcrops here making it an interesting area to explore. If you wish, you can make this a longer walk by simply continuing further south along the road, then backtracking. It's unlikely that you will meet many vehicles. We did meet a group of cyclists from Guanajuato touring along the trail.

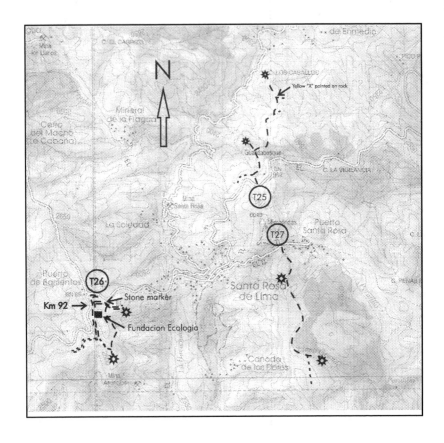

Route 28: Hoya Rincon de Parangueo

Time: 3 to 4 hours return
Distance: 4 kilometers
Difficulty: Easy to Strenuous
Hazards: Steep trail and loose rock on ascent to view petroglyphs
Elevation Change: 100 meters
Topo Map: None needed
Attractions: Tunnel; extinct volcanic crater; petroglyphs

Accessing the trail: This little jewel is about a one and a half hour drive south of Guanajuato City. From the city, drive south taking the free road Mex 45 to Irapuato and Salamanca. This route takes you through the famous strawberry growing region of the state. Take the south by-pass around Salamanca and then follow Mex 43 south to Valle de Santiago. Upon entering Valle de Santaigo, you cross a railway track. Immediately after crossing the tracks, turn right and you will pick up the signs for Huanimaro. Follow the signs for Huanimaro which will lead you out to the west end of town. Leave the town and continue for another 7 kilometers heading west on the paved road. Take the first paved road to the right (north) which leads to the village of San Jose de Parangueo. Upon entering the village, take the first street to the right. Follow this street for about ½ km. Park your vehicle here.

Hoya Rincon Trail Locator Map

Walk up the dirt street to the point where it forks. Take the left fork. Walk along further for a block until you come to a small store on the left-hand side. Immediately past the store and on the left is a tunnel with the name "Rincon de Parangueo" above the tunnel entrance. The tunnel is about ½ km long. It is not lit, so you will need a flashlight or a candle and matches. You may be approached by young or teenage boys offering to guide you through the tunnel. If you wish, you can negotiate a price for their services. Once through the tunnel, you will emerge into the remains of an extinct volcanic crater. In the center are the remains of a small lake surrounded by a dazzling white clay-like material making it very bright under the mid-day sun. Follow along the eastern edge of the lake heading for the north side of the crater. Near a large tree along the north side of the crater are the words "Pinturas Rupestres" painted on two nearby rocks.

The trail up to the petroglyphs begins at the large tree well to the right of the painted rocks. Basically, the trail follows a steep dry wash up to the petroglyphs. The climb up is strenuous requiring at times the use of both hands and feet. It can become quite hot during the middle of the day so bring lots of water. The petroglyphs have been somewhat marred by modern graffitti but are still well worth the effort to see.

Crater and Lake from petroglyph site

San Louis Potosi State

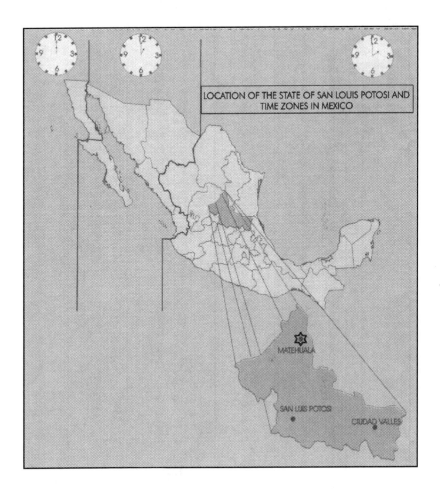

LOCATION OF THE STATE OF SAN LOUIS POTOSI AND TIME ZONES IN MEXICO

MATEHUALA

SAN LUIS POTOSI

CIUDAD VALLES

The two trails described here are easily accessible from the historic mining town of Real de Catorce which is surrounded by rolling hills and desert valleys.

Accessing the Area: From the north end of the city of Matehuala (using Las Palmas Hotel and Campground as a landmark) drive about 6 km north on Mex 57 to the junction of Mex 62. Turn left on Mex 62 and drive 18 km west to the town of Cedral. Once through Cedral, continue west for another 10 km. until you come to the junction of the road to Real de Catorce. This turnoff is well signed. Turn left and drive south for 25 km on a rough cobblestone road. Before reaching Real de Catorce there is a 2.3 km road tunnel suitable only for cars, pickup trucks and small busses. A small toll is charged and traffic is regulated as the tunnel is narrow and only one-way traffic is allowed. You may have to wait for up to 20 minutes before being allowed through. We never waited more than five minutes either way but during weekends, holidays or festivals it could take longer. Once through the tunnel you come to a large parking area. A small parking fee is charged. Don't try to drive into the town as the streets are narrow and very steep. Allow about 1.5 hours to drive to Real de Catorce or 2.5 hours by bus.

Real de Catorce Locator Map

There are two options with respect to accommodation. There are no campgrounds in Real de Catorce. RVers can stay at the Hotel La Siesta or the Motel Oasis in Matehuala and drive into Real de Catorce every day. A better option would be to drive or take a bus to Real de Catorce and stay in the town for a few days at one of the hotels or pensions. It's a great place to be after the tourists have left and the shops are closed. You can be easily transported back into the past when fortunes were being made and lost in this once prosperous mining town. When you exhaust the sights and sounds of the town, you can then walk one of the several trails that radiate out of the town following some of the old travel routes used back in the silver mining days. Two trails are described here.

Route 29: Cerro La Mision

Time: 3 hours
Distance: 7 km return
Difficulty: Moderate to difficult
Hazards: Steep trail in places; some loose rock; high altitude
Elevation Change: 500 meters
Topo Map: F-14-A-24 Real de Catorce
Attractions: View of the old town and the surrounding valleys; desert plants

When in the parking area, look at the top of the mountain just to the south which overlooks the parking area and the town. You will see a blue colored cross near the top (see picture in Route 30). This will be your initial destination. On the south side of the parking lot a dirt road leads off in a westerly direction past several occupied houses on both sides of the road. Walk down this road for about 10 minutes until you come to the last inhabited structure on the right-hand side. On the left-hand side of the road look for what appears to be splotches of white paint splashed on reddish colored rock [14Q 0307494; UTM 2620635]. Right above it are the remains of a building (two rock walls and part of a third). There is a small wash just to the left of these remains and a barbed wire fence running up the slope just to the left of the wash. Turn left off the road and scramble up along the right side of the wash. This will lead you up to a square rock and concrete water control structure[14Q 0307532; UTM 2620605]. Turn right at the water control structure and walk up the slope following a faint trail. In about 5 minutes you come to a fork in the trail [14Q 0307504; UTM 2620530]. Take the left fork and continue ascending. The trial is still a bit vague in places as it traverses over bare rock here; however, have faith as you will soon come upon a well defined foot path that becomes a series of six switchbacks. The first switchback is to the left [14Q 0307807; UTM2620437]. The last switchback is to the right [14Q 0308058; UTM2620399]. From here head towards the blue cross.

From the cross [14Q 0307973; UTM2620281] there are great views of the town below and the surrounding valley. Continue walking in a south-easterly direction to get to the top of Cerro La Mision (which is visible from the cross). Follow the faint trails through the open country to the top of Cerro La Mision [14Q 0308572; UTM 2619819]. From here there are some great views of the plains below to the east and west and the mountain ranges beyond. Looking back to where you came from you can just see the top of the blue cross. Return to the blue cross and pick up the trail back to town.

Overlooking Real de Catorce

Route 30: Real de Catorce to Cerro Quemado

Time: 5 hours return
Distance: 9 km return
Difficulty: Easy to Moderate
Hazards: High altitude; some loose rock on steeper section near end of trail
Elevation Change: 200 meters
Topo Map: F-14-A-24 Real de Catorce.
Attractions: Ruins of old mining operations and haciendas; spiritual center for the Huichol Indians; fantastic views from the top of Cerro Quemado; walk through desert vegetation

Follow the dirt road that leaves from the south side of the parking area and head in a westerly direction past several occupied houses. After about 10 minutes you leave the town. The trail follows along a stream below you and on your right [14Q 0307188; UTM 2620212]. The trail passes through a stone archway. Just after the archway it turns left, then right and begins climbing. You are now about 15 minutes into the walk. The trail continues to follow along the stream on the right.

The trail is now just a walking and horse trail. About 400 meters past the archway the trail forks. There are a couple of buildings at this point [14Q 0307360; UTM 2619815]. Take the right fork which heads immediately down through the dry stream bed and then up over a rise in a westerly direction. After about 400 meters there is another fork in the trail [14Q 0306982; UTM 2619874]. At this point you will probably be approached by someone with a receipt book who works for the local ejido (communal settlement). They charged 10 pesos for the use of the trail at the time that we walked it. Take the left fork and head for a blue sign that says that this is a protected area. At the blue sign the trail forks again. Go left. The trail follows an electrical line for a short while. Stay to the left of the only large tree visible. The trail goes over some dark red rock outcrop. Head for the next blue sign ahead on the trail. Cerro Quemado is now visible to the west. From the second blue sign [14Q 0306590; UTM 2619501] the trail drops down and crosses a wash; then forks again. Take the right fork which leads to a third blue sign at the top of a rise [14Q 0306267; UTM 2619415].

The trail continues on in a westerly direction and passes a fourth blue sign with a Huichol

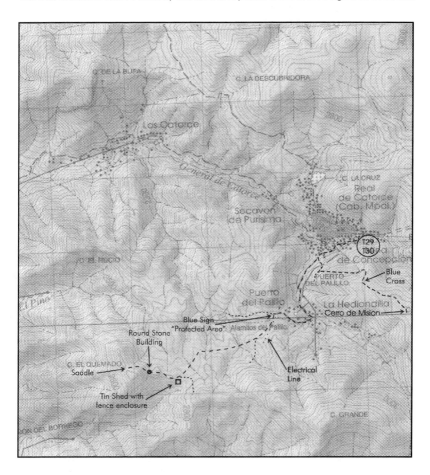

saying on it. Just past this sign the trail goes up over a rocky outcrop providing a good view of Cerro Quemado. Within another 200 meters the trail passes by a small barbed wire fence enclosure and an old tin shed, both on the left. Another trail joins up coming in from the left. You will see a fifth blue sign near this junction. About 100 meters past this junction the trail passes over a rocky knoll [14Q 0305552; UTM 2619045]. Another 275 meters further the trail passes by a round stone building with a flat roof [14Q 0305284; UTM 2619098]. This is a good place to pause for a rest and catch some shade before carrying on.

Once past the round stone building the trail ascends up to the saddle of Cerro Quemado [14Q 0304910; UTM 2619187]. On the saddle are the Hichol ceremonial circles. To the right and left you can walk to the top of the two hills on either side and get some magnificent views of the valley below including the railway towns of Estacion Catorce and Estacion Wadley as well as another mountain range off to the west and north. At the top of the hill on the left is a small building at which ceremonial offerings are left by the Huitchols. As this is a Huitchol spiritual site, please respect it and do not touch or remove any of the objects from the building.

Ruins left over from the old mining days

State of Colima

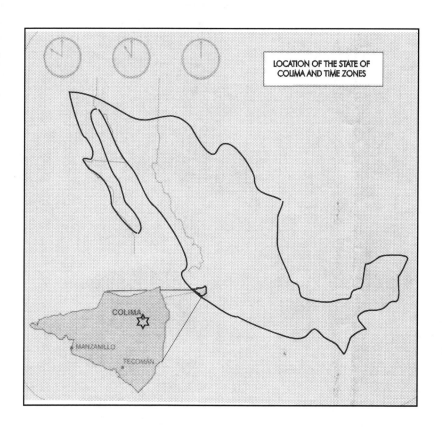

LOCATION OF THE STATE OF COLIMA AND TIME ZONES

The three trails described in this chapter are located in the beautiful hills and valleys found on the edge of an active volcano called Volcan de Colima, a short distance north of the city of Colima. This area is easily accessible by car or bus.

Colima Volcano Trails Route Map

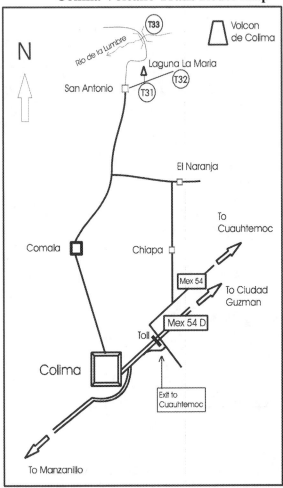

Accessing the Area: Take Mex 54 (four lane highway) heading north-east from Colima. In about 5 km from the outskirts of Colima take the free road by exiting the four lane highway on the right (before the toll booth) and then turning left and crossing over to the north side. The free road now parallels the toll road on it's north side. Shortly you will come to the turnoff for Chiapa. Chiapa is 5.5 km north of the turnoff and then it's another 8 km to the El Naranja junction.

At the junction turn left for San Antonio. In 6 km you come to another intersection. Turn right. At this intersection you will see signs advertising Laguna La Maria Tourist Center. Follow this road to San Antonio. Up to this point the road is paved. A couple of kilometers before getting to San Antonio the road turns to gravel but it is in good condition. At San Antonio there is another fork in the road. Take the right fork which takes you onto a cobblestone road. Follow it for about 1 km. The tourist center is on the left [13Q 0635817; UTM 2151877].

The Laguna La Maria Tourist Center: Within the tourist center there is a small lake called Laguna La Maria which is surrounded by treed hills. It is a beautiful location overlooking the lake and an active volcano not far away. At times during the night, when the volcano is more active, one can see lava running down its sides. During the day puffs of smoke and steam can be seen coming from the volcano with the occasional loud roar.

The tourist center has 5 small cabins or cottages for rent. The main building has a few rooms to rent as well as sinks and toilets for public use on the main floor. A restaurant and bar are located on the second floor. All these buildings are arranged in a circular fashion around a lawn with two pools - a small pool for children and a larger one for adults. A glassed in shelter is located just below the lawn with a view of the lake. There is a dirt road of about 0.5 km that goes from the center to the lake.

Along the lake shore there are picnic shelters and tables as well as small rowboats for rent. Fishing is also popular. This is a good area for birding. There is an 8.00 peso one time vehicle entry fee and a fee of 150.00 pesos for camping. If you are camping, electricity can be tapped out of the glassed in shelter or one of the other buildings. Showers are available in one of the rooms or cabins. There is 24 hour security.

Route 31: Laguna La Maria Trails

Time: 2.5 to 3 hours to enjoy the trails and the scene around the lake
Distance: 3 kilometers
Difficulty: Moderate to difficult
Hazards: High altitude; loose rock; eroded trails/landslides due to earthquake
Elevation Change: 140 meters
Topo maps: None needed. Trails are well marked
Attractions: Birds, tunnels, view of volcano

There are three short trails that can be accessed from around the lake. The tourist center describes them as Rutas 1, 2 and 3. Follow the dirt road to the lake. To get to Rutas 1 and 2, walk along the lake to the last set of two picnic shelters. Walk between the shelters and follow the path that goes along a barbed wire fence for a short time. On the other side of the fence is a small grove of coffee trees. Follow the path for about 10 minutes. The trail then branches right and left. The left branch is Ruta 1 which goes through three short tunnels. The trail ends at the end of the third tunnel. The trial used to go further but it was damaged by the earthquake in January of 2003. It is dangerous to go on any further.

Laguna La Maria

Return to the trail junction and head in the other direction. This is Ruta 2, although there is no sign indicating such. This trail goes through five short tunnels. After the fifth tunnel the trail virtually disappears due to a slide which has taken away the trail. You can see a sixth tunnel ahead but I advise not trying to go there as neither the trail nor the tunnel appear to be safe. Rutas 1and 2 should take you no more than an hour to do.

Ruta 3 is a little more challenging and we recommend using hiking boots for this one. It starts just after the first set of picnic tables on your right as you walk the road to the lake. There is a sign indicating the start of the trail. The last half of the trail is quite steep with rocks, roots and a few fallen trees along the way; however, you do get rewarded at the top with an impressive view of the volcano. It takes about a half hour to get to the top and about 15 minutes to come down. Allow yourself some time at the top to enjoy the scene.

Route 32: La Yerbabuena and the Mesa

Time: 7 hours
Distance: 10 kilometers
Difficulty: Moderate
Hazards: Some loose rock on the descent from the mesa into La Yerbabuena; high altitude
Elevation Change: 340 meters
Topo Maps: Comala E-13-B-34
Attractions: Spectacular views of the Colima del Fuego volcano

Note: About a dozen soldiers are stationed at Yerbabuena to monitor volcanic activity and, if necessary, shut the area down and evacuate the people. As long as the volcano is relatively quiet they will allow you to hike in the area. It is best to enquire at the tourist center first as to what the situation is like.

Starting from the entrance to the tourist center, turn left and follow the cobble stone road in a north-easterly direction towards the partly abandoned village of La Yerbabuena. This is a quiet road with very little traffic. It passes by fields and a few farms affording some initial views of the volcano. In About 2 km you will come to a military check point just outside the village of Yerbabuena. You'll need their permission to continue on to the Mesa. Just tell them that you are interested in walking up to the Mesa. They will let you know if it is safe to proceed. At the checkpoint a dirt road forks to the right off of the cobble stone road.

Take this right fork and within 20 meters or so pass through or around a gate. In 600 meters from the gate you will come to another fork in the two-track road [13Q 0638568; UTM 2153650]. Take the left fork. In about 100 meters the two-track road bends to the north and heads towards the escarpment [13Q 0638660; UTM 2154065]. The road then climbs over the escarpment bending back in an easterly direction. In about another kilometer the trail passes by a rusty metal gate on the left. It descends to the right with barbed wire fences on both sides. In about 200 meters you pass through a barbed wire gate. People do run cattle up here, so just be aware that you may have to make the odd detour to get around them. Once through the gate you find yourself in a large open meadow with a set of three abandoned buildings on a knoll in the middle [13Q 0638573; UTM 2154588]. This is a good place to stop for lunch.

After lunch return back to the rusty metal gate. Pass through the gate (which will

Colima volcano as seen from the trail

now be on your right) and follow the trial heading east. This is still a two-track trail of sorts. Within 500 meters of the rusty gate a footpath forks off to the left (south) [13Q 0637735; UTM 2154258]. Watch for a larger dark colored rock on the right-hand side of the double track trail. The footpath forks left shortly after this rock and quickly begins to descend the escarpment. This is a well used footpath in reasonably good condition which switchbacks down the escarpment. The trail drops about 120 meters in altitude to the base of the escarpment. Once at the bottom the trail levels out and passes by a corral-like structure on the right. Follow the trail that bends off to the left and then to the right past a tin shed. Once around the tin shed the trail becomes one of the streets of the village of Yerbabuena. This street will take you to the village plaza. Walk across the plaza and pick up the cobble stone road back for Laguna La Maria.

Route 33: Lugna Verde Trail

Time: 6 hours from trail head
Distance: 9 km return
Difficulty: Easy
Hazards: High altitude
Elevation Change: 320 meters
Topo Maps: E-13-B-34 Comala
Attractions: Walk through a small river valley; great views of the volcano; small farming operations; some birding

Accessing the trail: There are two ways to access the trailhead. From El Centro Turistico La Maria, turn right and walk back along the cobble stone road 1 km to the village of La Becerrera. At the intersection with the main dirt road, turn right and walk or hitch hike the 3 km to the new bridge over El Rio de la Lumbre. There is a fair amount of traffic going up this road so it shouldn't be too difficult to hitch a ride to the bridge. Another option would be to arrange a ride with the tourist center operators for a fee. Just after crossing the bridge, take the first dirt road heading off to the right. The road heads back down to the river. In a hundred meters or so you'll come to a barbed wire gate on your left and a two-track dirt road heading off in a north-easterly direction. This is the trailhead.

Note: At the time that we walked this trial the bridge was under construction. Hopefully this description of accessing the trial will be adequate providing the construction hasn't rearranged things too much. Basically the trail starts from the north side of the bridge and heads in a north-easterly direction with the river on the right.

Pass through the barbed wire gate (gate 1) and head up the two-track road. Within 200 meters the trail passes through another barbed wire gate (gate 2). In another 200 meters it passes through a metal gate (gate 3) [13Q 0636225; UTM 2154290]. In the next 1.5 km the trail passes through 5 more gates. Gate 4 is a barbed wire gate and gate 5 is a metal gate which is kept locked to keep out unwanted vehicle traffic. It is possible to crawl through the barbed wire fence on the right and pass through the wooden gate immediately to the right of the metal gate. Between gate 5 and gate 6 the trail passes by a couple of buildings that have people living in them. They farm the land around here.

The nice thing about this walk so far is that there are small water channels carrying water down from the hills for irrigation. It's possible to stop and dip your hat in the water or have a quick splash bath (clothes and all) to cool yourself off. Next is gate 7 [13Q 0637040; UTM 2155029]. From here, the trail passes through two more gates (gates 8 & 9). In between these two gates is a finca (small farm) with goats and other animals. We met two gentlemen here who were bagging maiz. Pass through the finca and gate 9 which is about 150 meters beyond it. Walking time between gate1 and the finca is 50 to 60 minutes. The GPS reading approximately 50 meters north of gate 9 is [13Q 0637536; UTM 2155220]. From here the trail passes through two more gates (gates 10 & 11).

Just past gate 11 [13Q 0637932; UTM 2155658] walkers begin to get some nice views of Volcan de Colima and the inactive but higher volcano Nevado de Colima behind it. 250 meters past gate 11 the trail forks [13Q 0638075; UTM 2155650]. The main trail forks to the right but it's worth a short side trip to the left for about 125 meters to a small corral and a view of the barranca. This is Laguna Verde.

Return to the main trail and continue heading east. In about 100 meters there is another fork in the trail. Keep right again. In the next 15 minutes the trail turns to the right, goes down through a dry stream bed, then up and to the left again, then climbs up and to the right passing through a wooden gate (gate12)[13Q 0638205; UTM 2155290]. The trail

View of volcano from Laguna Verde trail.

now passes through some taller trees, then swings to the left and passes through another barbed wire gate (gate 13) [13Q 0638163; UTM 2155050]. The trail now enters a clearing with a corn patch on a slope on the right and a small shelter directly ahead. Further to the right, just above the corn patch, is a knoll with a large tree near the top From the knoll [13Q 0638163; UTM 2155050] you are rewarded with a brilliant 360 degree view of the volcanoes and the surrounding volcanic landscape. From the wooden gate to this point takes about 15 minutes.

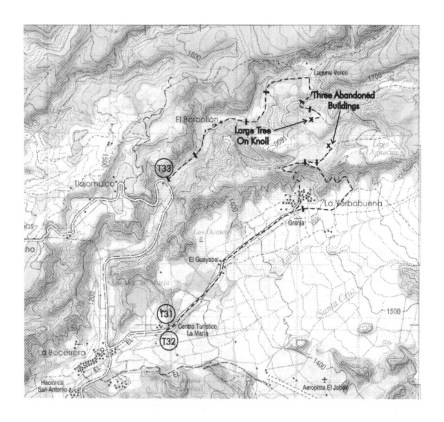

State of Nayarit

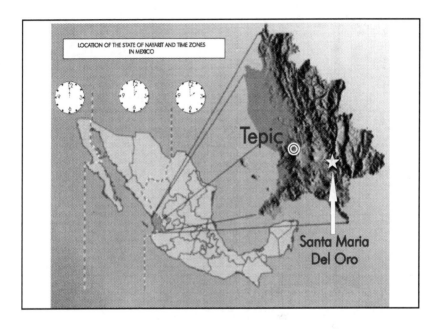

The three trails described in this chapter are located in and around a picturesque area called Laguna Santa Maria del Oro. This is a pleasant lake situated in an extinct volcanic crater surrounded by steep forested mountains. The lake is 2 km in diameter and has cold greenish-blue clear water. The forests that surround the lake are composed primarily of pine, encino and oak, and are home to a great variety of birds making this place a great birding area. It is also a popular recreation area for people from Tepic and Guadalajara and it can get busy on weekends and holidays. Otherwise, the place is usually very quiet. There are several restaurants strung out along the shoreline. Koala Bungalows and RV Park is located on the south shore of the lake and offers both rooms to rent and a trailer park for smaller rigs.

Accessing the Aaea: Head east from Tepic on Mex 15 for 4 km till you come to the junction of the toll road and the free road. From here you have the option of taking the toll road or the free road. We recommend taking the free road as it's more interesting and not very busy. Take the free road for 23.5 km heading south-east until you come to a road junction. Turn north-east and pass over the toll road following the signs for Santa Maria del Oro 10.6 km ahead. Pass through the town of Santa Maria del Oro and continue for another 2.8 km to the crater rim where there is a viewpoint with a parking area. The next 6.8 km is a steep descent to the lake. Upon arriving at the lake there is a T-junction. Turn left and follow the short dirt access road to Koala Bungalows and RV Park.

Laguna de Maria del Oro Locator Map

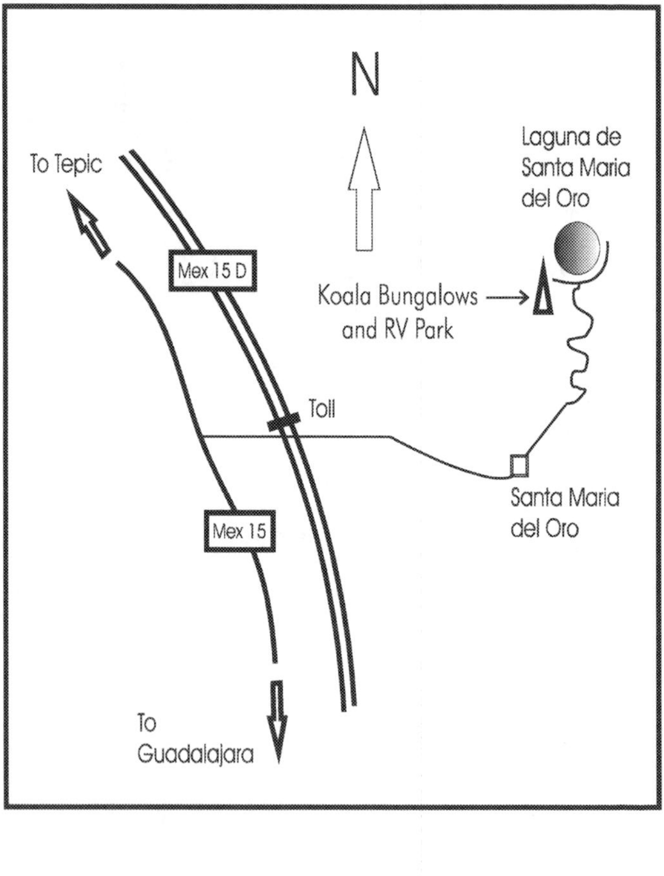

N

To Tepic

Mex 15 D

Laguna de Santa Maria del Oro

Koala Bungalows ⟶ and RV Park

Toll

Mex 15

Santa Maria del Oro

To Guadalajara

Route 34: Around the Lake Walk

Time: 4 hours
Distance: 8 km
Difficulty: Easy
Hazards: None
Elevation Change: None
Topo Maps: F-13-D-32 Santa Maria del Oro
Attractions: Birds; butterflies; large trees; lake views

Starting from the Koala Bungalows and RV Park [13Q 0544184; UTM 2361968] walk over to the small reception building. Pass to the left of it and then past a house just behind it. Once past the house a footpath meanders along the lakeshore passing through several gates and fence stiles. In about 30 minutes the trail comes out onto a dirt road. Keep right following the dirt road for about 15 minutes until you come to a fork in the road with a rough wooden sign indicating the way to "La Selva Restaurant". Take the left fork and in another 10 minutes or so you'll come to another sign for "La Selva Restaurant" with an access road heading off to the right to the restaurant [13Q 0543485; UTM 2363043]. Continue straight ahead until you come to another fork in the road. The right fork has a sign that says,"Camino Cerrado". This is a private road. Take the left fork which is signed,"Camino Vecinal".

The road undulates past many private lakeside cottages and properties. Within 45 minutes you'll pass by the Santa Maria Resort - a luxury resort. It's worth stopping in just to see the layout. In another 5 minutes or so along the road you'll pass by El Desague Restaurant. This is a good place to stop and take a break. They have fish and shrimp dinners as well as cold

Trail follows shoreline of lake

beer and drinks. All this comes with a nice view of the lake. From here the road continues south and then swings east around the south-east corner of the lake, passing several more restaurants along the lakeshore. About 1 km east of Koala there is an abarrote on the left-hand side of the road where one can pick up some water, milk and a few fruits and vegetables. To return to Koala, follow the road along the lake past the T-junction and along the access road back to the bungalows and trailer park.

Route 35: Ruta La Quebrada

Time: 7 hours
Distance: First portion: 6 km return; total trail: 10 km
Difficulty: First part of trail is easy to moderate; second portion is moderate to difficult and only for the more adventurous
Hazards: Some loose rock on trail; some dry stream bed and boulder hopping on second portion
Elevation Change: 200 meters
Topo Maps: F-13-D-32 Santa Maria del Oro
Attractions: Great views of the lake and surrounding coutryside; rock outcrops; vulture roosting sites

The directions for the first part of this trial are the same as for Route 34 until you get to the second sign and access road for La Selva Restaurant. Opposite the access road to the restaurant (just before the road crosses the dry stream bed) there is a footpath heading up to the left of the road through a barbed wire gate [13Q 0543485; UTM 2363043]. The trail immediately begins to climb through and around some larger boulders. In a minute or so the trail crosses the dry stream bed and climbs up the other bank. Within about 20 meters there is a trail that comes in from the right. Just ignore this trail as it just goes back down to the road. Continue straight ahead. The trail is in good condition at this point and easy to follow. The trail now skirts along the right side of the stream. Within a minute or so you will notice a 4-inch metal water pipe crossing the stream. You'll come to a place where the pipe has been disconnected and a piece laying off to one side and a large boulder on the right-hand side of the stream.

At this point it is a little confusing as to where the trail really goes. As you face the big boulder with a tree growing out of its right side, keep to the right of the boulder and you'll pick up the trail again. The trail continues to climb along the stream and past another large boulder on your right. As this is a well-treed area it is a little difficult to follow the trail at times due to the large amount of dead leaves on the ground which makes the surface all look alike. You just have to keep your eyes peeled to see where the trail is. Within about 5 minutes the trail crosses a dry stream that comes down from the right. You should be about 1 hour into the hike at this point. Its difficult to take any GPS readings through here due to the heavy tree canopy, however, there is lots of shade which makes it cooler for hiking.

After crossing the stream that comes down from the right, the trail follows along the left side of this stream, then continues to climb steadily with short switchbacks. There are some rocks and larger stones on the trail. In about 30 minutes the trail comes out to an opening affording a great view of the lake to the east [14Q 0542965; UTM 2363398]. Pass through the barbed wire gate and immediately cross a dry stream. The trail swings up to the left, then circles around to the right around a knoll [13Q 0542929; UTM 2363330]. Soon the trail begins following a barbed wire fence and a small stream, both on the left-hand side. As you walk along, you'll notice some open hillsides off to the right. In about 10 minutes from the knoll, the trail passes through a barbed wire fence with a wooden gate [13Q 0542626; UTM 2363554]. In another 5 minutes it comes out to an agricultural area. There is a metal gate with a building on the left. A dirt road continues west beyond the metal gate. From here one gets nice views of the valley and hills to the west as well as views of fields of aguave, cane and maize. It is recommended that the walker turn around at this point and return to the area of the knoll. This walk from the knoll to the metal gate and back is a very pleasant hike with trees and shade along the trial and should only take about a half hour. At this point walkers have the option of returning back to the road and Koala on the same path that they came in on or forging on.

For the next part of the walk it is recommended that one wear proper hiking boots, as at times there is no actual trail and a little bushwacking will be required. Walk around the knoll (which will now be on your left). Just before crossing the dry stream bed, if you look up to the left (north), you can see a high hill with some rock outcrop. There is no real trail up to the top but it is fairly open with numerous cattle trails which can be used. You might want to use the Go To function on your GPS to help you along using the next few readings to guide you to the top.

Strike off for the rock outcrop keeping other landmarks in view for reference. Upon getting to the first rise there are some great views of the valley and hills to the west and south [13Q 0543113; UTM 2363644]. Keep heading for the highest point. The walking gets easier as you go higher. Once on top it is quite open with some scattered trees making the walk quite easy [13Q 0543260; UTM 2364015]. There are great views all around. At this point you will be walking in a north-west direction. After several minutes the trail begins dropping down following a quebrada (dry stream) on the left. It is still easy walking with trees getting larger and more dense. There is a path evident here.

The trail, although rather faint, continues on to a ridge overlooking the lake [13Q 0543600; UTM 2364472]. The trail now drops down off the ridge to the left and comes out to a large open area. You want to pick up the quebrada (ravine) dropping down to the right and follow along the right side of this quebrada. You actually have to bear right and climb a little before getting to the beginning of the quebrada which leads down to the lake. From the top of the quebrada you can see the octogonal red roof of a building along the lake. Use that as your landmark. The first 15 minutes of the descent is through relatively open country. Then you come to a barbed wire fence. Beyond the fence the vegetation growth becomes quite thick and difficult to walk through. We recommend turning right and following along the fence until you pick up another quebrada coming down from the right. Look for a trail on the right-hand side of the quebrada and head down. If you don't pick it up right away, walk down the rocky stream bed. This makes for an interesting hike in and of its own. You should pick up the trail on the right within 10 or 15 minutes. Then, just follow the trail to the road keeping the quebrada on your left.

Eventually the trail exits onto the road [13Q 0544265; UTM 2364030] in front of a white house with a red tiled roof. Immediately to the left the quebrada crosses the road and passes through three large circular holes in a rock-wall fence. It takes about 45 minutes to come down from the top of the quebrada to the road. Once on the road, you can turn either right or left to return to Koala.

Rock ledge along trail overlooking lake

Route 36: Chichicastla Cascadas Trail

Time: 5-6 hours (allowing time to play in the pools, explore the stream and have lunch)
Distance: 10 km return
Difficulty: Easy to Moderate
Hazards: Cow pies and cattle
Elevation Change: 80 meters
Topo Maps: F-13-D-32 Santa Maria del Oro
Attractions: Waterfalls; views of the pastoral countryside; birds; stream exploring, swimming spots

From the Koala campground turn right and follow the entrance road back to the paved road. Follow the paved road east along the lake for about 800 meters. Just before reaching the school, watch for a trail heading up to the right [13Q 0545311; UTM 2361840] (almost directly opposite a metal gate leading into a park-like area along the lake attached to a restaurant). The walk from the campground to this point should take 15-20 minutes. Take this trail heading south which climbs a small hill. After a couple of minutes the trail forks. Take the left fork. The trail flattens out, then climbs a bit again [13Q 0545310; UTM

2361686]. In a few more minutes the trail reaches the top of the rise [13Q 0545455; UTM 2361542]. It now descends slightly and in several minutes it emerges onto a gravel road [13Q 0545488; UTM 2361445].

One of many rock pools found along the stream

It should take about 15 minutes from the paved lake road to the gravel road. There are some farm buildings just across the road. This road runs roughly in an east-west direction with the Rio Chichicastla running along the south side of the road. Turn left and head east down the road for 1 km. This should take 20-25 minutes.

You'll come to a point where the stream crosses over the road. Just before crossing the stream, look for a two-track trail which branches left off the gravel road [13Q 0546769; UTM 2361872]. Branch left following this two-track trail heading in a north-easterly direction. In about 400 meters the trail passes over a rise offering some nice views of the surrounding hills, valleys and farmlands. [13Q 0547141; UTM 2362300]. There are fence lines on both sides and the stream is just off to the east side of the trail. In another 200 meters the trail passes through a barbed wire gate. Carrying on for several more minutes you will begin to notice rocky cliffs off to the right of the trail and the stream [13Q 0547683; UTM 2362783].

In another 100 meters or so there is another barbed wire gate [13Q 0547600; UTM 2362867]. This gate is about a 30 minute walk from branching off the gravel road. Pass through this gate, then immediately turn right and take the footpath that follows a barbed wire fence on the right-hand side. It's about another 15 minutes from here to the falls. The footpath first heads in an easterly direction, then swings south continuing to follow the fence line. Where the trail starts heading south, there is a water pipe on the left-hand side of the trail. In another 10 minutes or so the trail drops down gradually to the beginnings of the falls. There are many nice drops and pools along this part of the stream where walkers can take a refreshing dip after what can be a hot walk in the sun. From here, the stream drops rapidly through the rocks.

Stream walking option: We've been told that it is possible to walk along the stream bed starting from where the stream crosses the gravel road [13Q0546769; UTM 2361872] to the top of the falls [13Q 0547741; UTM 2362401] using Tevas or water tennies as foot gear. We haven't tried this route but Vince at Koala Bungalows assures us it's quite "doable" and lots of fun.

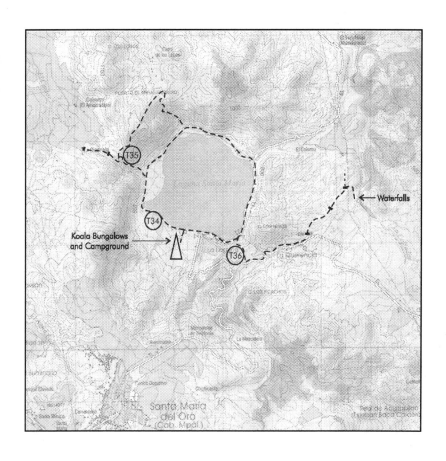

State of Chihuahua

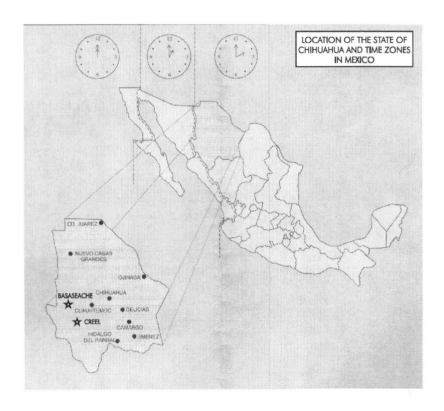

Seven trails are described for this state. Five are located around the town of Creel which is a popular tourist destination for North Americans and Europeans. The other two trails are found in Baseseachi National Park located north-west of Creel.

Accessing Creel: Creel is located 250 km by road south-west of the city of Chihuahua. From the city of Chihuahua, take Mex 16 west for 164 km passing through the city of Cuauhtemoc. The turnoff for Creel is located 62 km west of Cuauhtemoc. Turn south at the junction and drive for another 86 km to Creel. This road is paved and in good condition. Creel has a variety of accommodations ranging from guesthouses for hikers and backpackers to comfortable motel/hotel rooms. The Villa Mexicana (KOA) Campground and Cabins is located on the south-east edge of the town, about a 15-20 minute walk from the town center. Access to all trails will be described as beginning from this campground.

Creel Trails Locator Map

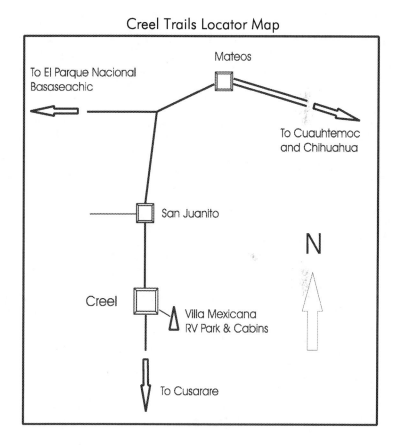

Route 37: The Valley of the Monks

Distance: 16 km return
Time: 6-7 hours return
Difficulty: Easy to moderate
Hazards: High altitude; Can be dusty in high winds
Elevation Change: Very little
Topo Maps: G-13-A-22 Creel
Attractions: Unusual rock formations; small villages

From the entrance to the Villa Mexicana Campground [13R 0240195; UTM 3071107], walk south for about 2 minutes till you come to a fork in the streets. Just past the "Mini Super Amador" a paved street forks to the right and leads up to the highway. The other street is dirt and goes straight ahead. Continue straight ahead on the dirt street. After about another 2 minutes (just past the lumber operation on the right-hand side) the dirt street forks. Take the left fork that goes past the cemetery. You are now on a dirt road that leads out of town. In about 5 minutes you'll come to a toll booth where the local ejido collects a small fee from tourists using their trails.

In just over a kilometer from the toll booth there is a trail that branches off to the right [13R 0241965; UTM 3069878] with a sign that says, "Bienbenido Valle de los Hongos" with an arrow pointing to the right and "Bienbenido Valle de los Monges a 6 km " with an arrow pointing left. The trail branching right leads to the Valley of Mushrooms just 200 meters or so off the road. What you do here is walk in and take a look at the unusual formations, then come back to the main dirt road.

Just ahead is the little settlement of San Ignacio with its small church, school and several houses scattered about. Continue walking on the dirt road that passes to the left of the village. Within a kilometer past the village there is a footpath heading off to the left [13R 0243532; UTM 3070343]. By taking this footpath you can return to Creel. However, to continue on to the Valley of the Monks, continue walking east down the dirt road. In just over another kilometer you'll come to a dirt track branching off to the right with reddish-orange arrows on fence posts pointing off to the right [13R 0244383; UTM 3069906]. Don't take this branch, but carry on straight ahead (east). 400 meters further is a bridge over a small stream. Just before the bridge a dirt track branches to the right. Continue over the bridge and straight ahead for about another 150 meters to where the road forks again [13R 0245051; UTM 3069617]. The main road forks up to the right over a small rise. The left fork is a lesser used dirt track heading straight on. You can take either fork as they meet up again at the top of the rise.

Another 2.5 km further on is the little village of Gonogchi. Just before entering the village the road forks [13R 0247034; UTM 3069551]. From this fork in the road a school building can be seen off to the right. Take the left fork and follow the dirt track for another kilometer which takes you into the Valley of the Monks. Here one can go and ramble among the strange rock formations.

You can return to Creel by the same route you came in on. An alternative way to return to Creel is to take the footpath that was noted earlier in the route description at GPS reading [13R 0243532; UTM 3070343] (just over a kilometer east of San Ignacio). Turn right onto this foot path which quickly joins up with a dirt track. Follow the dirt track for a short distance till you come to a fork in the dirt tracks [13R 0243104; UTM 3070784]. Take the narrow concrete bridge across the stream and follow the foot path up the rock hill. About 700 meters along this foot path another footpath joins from the left [13R 0242471; UTM 3071137]. There is red paint on a tree and a rock at this junction. There is a blaze on a tree just ahead. This trail is well used and easy to follow. Within the next 1.3 km you come to the highest point along the trail [13R 0241171; UTM 3071934]. From here you can see the town of Creel spread out down below. The trail now drops down and eventually joins with

a dirt track coming up from the left. Turn left and follow the dirt track down to Creel. When you get to the bottom of the dirt track, take the first street to the left which is a short street, right onto another dirt street, left onto a short paved street which takes you onto a wider paved street. Turn right. This street takes you out to the main streets of the town: Calle Elfido Batista and Avenida Lopez Mateos.

Rock formations in Valley of the Monks

Route 38: Rukiraso Waterfall and Lookout Point

Distance: 15 kilometers return
Time: 7 hours
Difficulty: Easy to Moderate
Hazards: High altitude; unprotected precipices at Rukiraso Falls and Lookout Point.
Caution is urged.
Elevation Change: Very little
Topo Maps: G-13-A-22 Creel
Attractions: Nice walk through pine forests and spectacular views overlooking Rukiraso
Waterfall and the canyon carved out by the Arroyo San Ignacio

From the entrance to the Villa Mexicana Campground [13R 0240195; UTM 3071107], walk south for about 2 minutes till you come to a fork in the streets. Just past the "Mini Super Amador" a paved street forks to the right and leads up to the highway. The other street is dirt and goes straight ahead. Continue straight ahead on the dirt street. After about 2 minutes (just past the lumber operation on the right-hand side) the dirt street forks. Take the right fork. This becomes a dirt road that heads south out of town paralleling the highway. In about 1 km the dirt road passes what appears to be a water aeration system located on the stream just to the right of the trail. In about another kilometer the trail passes under the highway bridge and crosses over to the right-hand side of the stream. You might have to get your feet wet here. Once out from under the bridge, the trail heads up to the right where it joins with a two-track trail [13R 0240924; UTM 3069369]. Turn left here and follow the two-track trail which heads off in a southerly direction. The two-track trail enters a pleasant little valley bordered by pine trees on either side and follows along a stream on the left. Follow this two-track trail for about 3.5 km where there is a fork in the trail [13R 0239816; UTM 3065768]. Note the pile of boulders just off to the left by the stream. Take the right fork which heads up into the pine forest. Once the trail enters the forest, it climbs steeply along an eroded 4-wheel drive track for about 300 meters and then begins to level out. Just before the trail levels out, it forks [13R 0239817; UTM 3065377]. Look for a tree at this junction with an orange blaze paint spot on it. Take the right fork. Go up this two-track trail for about 150 meters until you come to another fork in the trail. Note another tree at this fork with a red paint blaze marker. Take the left fork and follow this two-track trail for about 100 meters. Here another trail joins from the left, then the trail almost immediately forks again. Note the blaze (not painted) on the tree at this fork. Take either fork as these two trails join up again about 200 meters ahead. Once at the point where the trails re-join [13R 0239380; UTM 3064979], note the red blaze on the tree to the right-hand side of the joining trails. Within 50 meters the trail forks again. Take the right fork. In just over 300 meters from this fork the trail forks again [13R 0239338; UTM 3064610]. The two-track trail branches to the left. A foot path heads off straight ahead. Note the red blaze on a tree just 25 meters back from this junction on the left-hand side of the trail.

Take the left fork following the two-track trail which quickly turns into a wide walking path. Note a blazed tree about 30 meters ahead on the left fork. In about 200 meters a foot path comes in from the left to join the trail. Continue on the wide foot path for another 800 meters until the trail emerges onto the promontory which projects into the canyon. The trail follows along the top of the promontory allowing views of the canyon off both sides. In about 200 meters after emerging onto the promontory, there is a short trail jogging off to the left [13R 0239995; UTM 3063816] which leads to a spectacular view of the Rukiraso Waterfall. From here the trail continues on for another 400 meters out to the end of the promontory and another viewpoint offering a fantastic view of the canyon and the Recowata Hot Springs 1.5 km to the south. **Extreme caution should be taken here as there are no guard rails to protect people from the dangerous precipices.**

Route 39: Recowata Viewpoint

Distance: 12 kilometers return
Time: 6 hours
Difficulty: Moderate
Elevation Change: 340 meters
Topo Maps: G-13-A-22 Creel
Attractions: Rock outcrops, pine forests, small farms, and canyon views

Accessing the Trailhead: From the entrance to Villa Mexicana Campground drive 6.4 km south of Creel to the artesania shop located just before km 98 on the east side of the highway at Lake Arareko. The trail begins across the highway from the artesania shop.

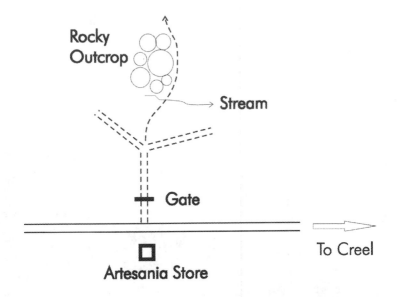

Rocky Outcrop

→ **Stream**

+ **Gate**

□
Artesania Store

⇒ **To Creel**

From the artesania shop, cross the highway and take the dirt track heading in a south-westerly direction. Pass through the gate and almost immediately (by an electrical utility pole) the dirt track forks with a footpath heading up the middle. Take the footpath which crosses a small stream and heads around to the right of the rocky outcrop just ahead. Go around the rocky outcrop, drop down through another stream and up the other side, then bear slightly to the left and head for the next obvious rock outcrop on a ridge. The trail passes by a residence on the right just before reaching the rock outcrop. The trail goes up over the rock outcrop [13R 0243745; UTM 3066324], then traverses along the left side of the ridge for 200+ meters [13R 0243756; UTM 3066105].

In another 100 meters the trail levels out coming to a 3-way fork [13R 0243695; UTM 3066035]. Take the middle trail. Within 200 meters the footpath intersects and crosses a two-track trail [13R 0243543; UTM 3065866]. A few meters ahead the path crosses another two-track trail. Proceed straight ahead on the footpath. Within a minute the trail crosses over a small rocky wash. Once past the wash, the path forks. Take the left fork. In another minute the path passes by a house and some wooden fences on the right. A path forks off to the right to the house. Keep left on the main footpath. About 30+ meters beyond the house and fences the trail forks [13R 0243422; UTM 3065658]. Take the right fork. Within a few minutes the path comes out onto a two-track trail coming in from the left [13R 0243411; UTM3065472].

Keep right and follow the two-track trail over and down the hill heading in a south-east direction. The trail passes by some buildings, a fence and some cultivated land on the left. Shortly, another two-track road comes in from the left. Bear right and proceed straight ahead. Within a few meters this two-track trail joins with another two-track trail coming in from the left. Turn right here and you will come out at a fence and a cultivated field on the right [13R 0243424; UTM 3065166]. Follow the trail that parallels the fence.

In about 50 meters the trail comes out onto another, better used two-track road. Note the fenced in farm just as you come onto this better used two-track road. Turn left and follow the two-track road as it skirts around the farm to the right following the fence line heading in a southerly, then a south-westerly direction. Follow the two-track trail to the end of the fence line [13R 0243039; UTM 3064528].

A foot path heads off straight ahead following along the right side of a small stream. About 200 meters down the path there is a small stone bridge over the stream. Cross over to the left hand side of the stream and continue following the path heading downstream. Within another 100 meters the trail passes a tree with a blaze on it [13R 0242826; UTM 3064183]. The stream on the right is now dropping quickly. The path now leaves the stream and in 100 meters the foot path intersects with another trail [13R 0242725; UTM 3064112]. Cross this trail and proceed straight ahead. In about 100 meters from this trail crossing, the trail forks. Take the left fork. As you proceed, the trail begins to drop gradually [13R 0242470; UTM 3063865]. Here the trail is wide and in good condition affording glimpses of the canyon ahead. In another 100 meters or so the trail forks [13R 0242245; UTM 3063647]. Keep left following the trail with blazes on two trees ahead.

The trail drops quickly over some rocky terrain and joins a two-track trail at a stream and a fence [13R 0242075; UTM 3063465]. Turn right and follow the two-track trail keeping the stream on your left. Within 50 meters there is a house on the right. In another 100 meters the trail crosses the stream and follows along its left side. Within 25 meters the trail re-crosses the stream back over to the right side [13R 0241641; UTM 3063587]. Here there are fenced-in cultivation plots on the right and left. The trail continues between these plots and up the hill directly ahead. Follow the trail till you get to the top of the hill with a small clearing [13R 0241306; UTM 3063667]. Note the burned forest on the left. Turn left and

View from edge of canyon

follow a two-track trail through the burned forest. Watch for blazes on the burned standing trees. Some of the trees have fallen so it is necessary to walk around or over them. Eventually the two-track trail leaves the burned over area [13R 0241072; UTM 3063466]. Within 200 meters the trail branches off to the right from the two-track trail [13R 0240871; UTM 3063278] and accesses the promontory. From here there are no real defined trails but one can just ramble along the edge of the promontory and appreciate the incredible views of the canyon. There is relatively little undergrowth which makes walking easy. You can walk around to the southern end of the promontory which overlooks the canyon and the Recowata Hot Springs to the south. **Exercise extreme caution as there are no guardrails to protect people from the dangerous precipices.**

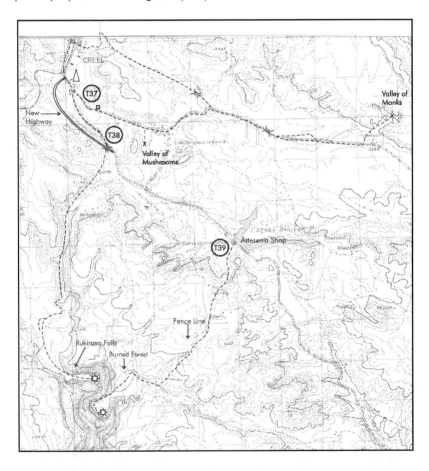

Route 40: Cusarare Waterfall

Distance: Access 1: 6 km return
Access 2: 6 km return
Time: 4 hours from either trail head to the falls
Difficulty: Easy
Hazards: High altitude
Elevation Change: 100 meters
Topo Maps: G-13-A-22 Creel
Attractions: Interesting walk through pine forests along boulder strewn streams and rocky outcorps; beautiful waterfall

Accessing the Trail: There are two places where the walker can access this trail:
Access 1: This access is located 16.7 km south of the Villa Mexicana Campground entrance in Creel (at the Km 108 marker on the highway). This is the Ramamuchi entrance which has an artesania shop and a parking area. This access is signed off the highway. There is a charge of 15 pesos by the local ejido to walk the trail.
Access 2: This access is located 20.6 km south of the Villa Mexicana Campground entrance (3.9 km south of Access 1). There is a hotel, artesania shop and a parking area. This access is also signed off the highway.

Access 1: From the artesania shop head over to the toll booth located along the two track trail just a couple of minutes walk north-west of the artesania shop. After passing through the toll, continue on the two-track trail which crosses over to the left side of the stream. After several minutes of walking, the two-track trail crosses back through some boulders to the right side of the stream [13R 0247390; UTM 3058976]. In about 200 meters the trail forks [13R 0247292; UTM 3058777]. Take the right fork. Note the white arrow painted on a rock on the right-hand side of the trail. The trail now becomes a footpath on the right-hand side of the stream. The two-track trail crosses the stream to the left. About 300 meters further on the two-track trail re-joins the footpath but ends here [13R 0247132; UTM 3058400]. There is a shelter off to the right of the trail.

Just ahead is a sign on a tree which reads, "Se prohibe cortar, remover, o sacar pinos". The footpath continues on past this sign along the right side of the stream. At this

Cusarare Falls during dry season

point you are about a half hour into the walk. For the next 15 minutes the trail continues along the right side of the stream. It's very pretty through here. The stream channel is strewn with large boulders and surrounded by large pine trees. The trail then crosses over to the left side of the stream on a log bridge. In another minute or so you come to the junction of the Arroyo Naqueachi (which you have been following up to this point) and the Rio Cusarare. There is a foot bridge that crosses the river and takes you over to the left side of Rio Cusarare.

The trail now joins up with the trail coming down from Access 2. Turn right here. The falls is 800 meters down this trail which follows along the left side of Rio Cusarare. Cusarare Falls is a is a beautiful scenic spot to spend some time and just appreciate the area. Several of the local Tarahumara ladies will be found around the falls area selling their crafts. They are very low key about it and you won't find yourself being hassled to buy things.

Access 2: The alternate trail access starts at the Hotel and artesania shop. Here again you have to pay the toll and then take the two-track trail that follows along the Arroyo Cusarare. In about 2 km the two-track trail crosses over to the right side of the stream [13R 0247066; UTM 3057408]. At this point a footpath branches off staying on the left side of the stream. Take the footpath as it is more pleasant than walking on the road surface. In about 500 meters the trail comes to the bridge crossing the Arroyo Cusasare and connecting to the trail coming down from Access 1. The falls are located 800 meters further down the trail which skirts along the left side of the river as you head downstream.

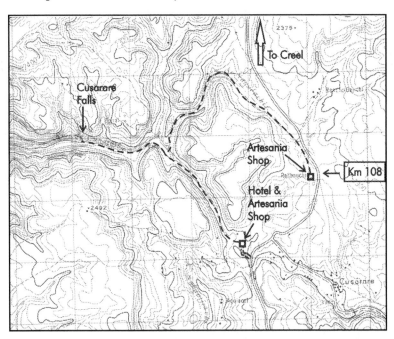

Route 41: Baseseachi Falls Trails

Accessing Baseseachi: Baseseachi is located 265 km by road west of the city of Chihuahua. From the city of Chihuahua, take Mex 16 west for 91 km passing through the city of Cuauhtemoc. The turnoff for Creel is located 62 km west of Cuauhtemoc. It is another 112 km from the Creel turnoff to Baseseachi on Mex 16. Just a few kilometers before getting to the village of Baseseachi take the paved road that branches to the left. There is a blue sign with an RV camping symbol directing you to Rancho San Lorenzo. Follow this road for a few kilometers. It will take you to the Rancho San Lorenzo cabins and camping area [12R 0775003; UTM 3118432]. It is possible to rent cabins here or dry camp. Water is available from the central building as well as flush toilets. At the time we visited they were in the process of installing an RV camping area complete with sewer and water. This may be in operation by the time of your visit.

Basaseachi Trails Locator Map

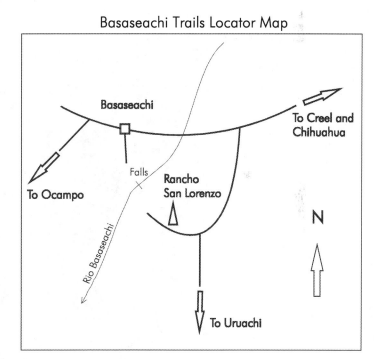

Accessing the Trail: From the Rancho San Lorenzo site entrance, turn right and walk up the paved road to El Divisidero. Within 15 minutes you will come to the parking area and vendor stalls. The trail begins here.

Distance: 8 km return
Time: 6 hours including going to the base of the falls
Difficulty: Easy to strenuous depending on which trails are walked.
Hazards: High altitude; some loose rock on steep sections
Elevation Change: 300 meters
Topo Maps: H-12-D-89 San Isidoro Huajumar.
Attractions: Breathtaking views of Baseseachi Falls and the Barranca Candamenia, swimming in waterfall pool

Pass through the vendor stalls and follow the concrete steps down to a fork in the trail and a set of signs which direct you to Divisidero and Divisidero II. These are viewpoints which give you fantastic views of Baseseachi Falls and the Barranca Candamenia. El Divisidero is the main viewing platform to which most people walk to view the falls; however, if you take the left fork, this trail will take you to Divisidero II and Divisidero III which are two different viewpoints located 700 meters down this trail which descends rapidly into the canyon. After about 100 meters you'll come to another sign directing you to Divisideros 2 and 3. In another 200 meters [12R 0774069; UTM 3118819] there is another sign directing you to Divisidero III. The trail forks here. Take the left fork. In about 5 minutes you will come out to Divisidero III viewpoint [12R 0773860; UTM 3118911] which offers great views of the falls and canyon. From here return to the last fork in the trail and turn left for Divisidero II. Divisidero II [12R 0774027; UTM 3118871] offers similar views of the falls from a slightly different angle.

Now backtrack to the first set of signs just past the set of concrete steps leading down from the vendor stalls and parking area. At this point turn left and head for Divisidero I. On the way you will see a sign for La Ventana with a trail heading off to the right. Ignore this for now and continue on to

Basaseachi Falls from Divisidero viewpoint

Divisidero I [12R 0774098; UTM 3118929] which is the highest point from which to view the falls and canyon.

After taking in all the fine views, backtrack about 50 meters and pick up the trail for La Ventana which now branches off to your left. Turn left and follow the La Ventana trail. In about 5 minutes you'll come to another fork in the trail [12R0774164; UTM 3119095]. The left fork is signed for La Ventana. La Ventana is another viewpoint about 1 kilometer down this trail which gets you a closeup look of the falls from below. The right fork is the upper trail which follows the canyon ridge to the top of Baseseachi Falls.

The La Ventana route drops down rapidly into the canyon. You can see the change in vegetation as you drop down. Within 35 minutes of walking there is another fork in the trail. The left fork takes you down to the La Ventana viewpoint. The right fork, signed to Baseseachi, takes you up to join the ridge trail. Take the left fork and head for La Vantana which is about 10 minutes down the trail and offers an interesting view of the falls from below. From here you have the option of following the trail which continues on down to the left of the concrete steps. If you follow this trail for another 15-20 minutes, it will take you to the pool at the bottom of the falls. Here there are some huge rocks and boulders to ramble over, as well as a pool in which to have a refreshing dip. It's a dramatic sight to watch the water cascading down over the lip of the canyon for 246 meters into the pool.

Now backtrack up the trail past the La Ventana viewpoint and back to the fork in the trail with the sign directing you to Baseseachi Falls. Take the left fork and keep climbing till you intersect with the ridge trail. The left fork takes you down to the top of the falls which is well worth a visit. The right fork takes you back to Divisadero I and the parking area. From the top of the falls one gets a panoramic view of the canyon. From here there is a well used trail that heads north to the left of the stream. This trail leads to another parking area about 500 meters ahead with more vendor stalls and a camping area run by the national park. Camping is free and water is available but there is no electricity. It is basically a tent or dry camp situation for small vans or campers.

Return to Divisidero I and the south parking area by backtracking and taking the ridge trail. After the initial climb back up from the top of the falls, the ridge trail is relatively level and is an enjoyable walk back.

Route 42: Barranca Candamania Viewpoint.

Distance: 10 km return
Time: 6 hours.
Difficulty: Moderate.
Hazards: High altitude; some loose rock on trail; high altitude; steep precipices at end of trail
Elevation Change: 300 meters.
Topo Maps: H-12-D-89 San Isadoro Huajumar
Attractions: Walk through pine and oak forests; superb views of the Barranca Candamenia and Baseseachi Falls in the distance

From the entrance to Rancho San Lorenzo [12R 0775003; UTM 3118432], turn left and walk along the paved road to the sign that says, "Bienvenido Rancho Ecoturistico San

Lorenzo" with two red Lobo arrows attached to the posts. Turn right here and follow the dirt road that immediately passes through a barbed wire gate and cattle guard. Immediately, on the left-hand side of the road, is a low rock outcrop. Walk along this for about 30+ meters until you pick up the beginning of the fence on your left. Climb over the fence and pass by the corral on the right. Then drop down over a small knoll, cross a small stream and pick up the two-track trail (brecha) heading up the hill ahead of you and to the right.

Once on the dirt track [12R 0774988; UTM 3117928], you will note the ranch house and cabins off to the right. Within another few minutes the trail passes through a barbed wire gate (about 15 minutes into the walk). The trail now follows a fence line on the right. In another 5 minutes or so there is a 3-pronged fork in the dirt track [12R 0775076; UTM 3117454]. Note the red Lobo arrow tacked to a tree pointing to the right. Take the right fork. About 15 minutes further along there is a fence on the right and rock outcrops ahead [12R 0774700; UTM 3117499] (about 35 minutes into the walk). In another 5 minutes the trail forks [12R 0774490; UTM 3117465]. Note the red Lobo arrow pointing to the left. Take the left fork. About 100 meters ahead the trail forks again [12R 0774449; UTM 3117321]. Take the right fork. Note the rock outcrops on the right. In 5 minutes or so you will come to a shelter (**Shelter 1**) with a metal roof [12 R 0774340; UTM 3117231] (50 minutes into the walk). The trail climbs for another minute, then swings off to the left. Note the red arrow on the tree ahead pointing left. The trail now switchbacks up the hill for a short while.

The trail now tops out [12R 0774165; UTM 3117120]. Note the red arrow on the left and the black arrow on the right pointing ahead (one hour into the walk). The trail now becomes a foot and horse trail which drops slightly, then climbs and begins to switchback. About 10 minutes from the last reading, there is another arrow nailed to a tree on the left side of the

View of Barranca Candamania

trail [12R 0773876; UTM 3116818]. From here one gets a great view overlooking the canyon on the right. The village of Baseseachi can be seen off in the distance. The road and north parking area for the falls can be seen from here. A few minutes past this point there is another shelter (**Sherlter 2**) with a metal roof and a fork in the trail [12R 0773832; UTM 3116610].

There is a sign indicating a Mirador 1,600 meters to the right of the shelter. Take the right fork. About 150 meters past the shelter is a viewpoint looking down into the Piedra Volada canyon [12R 0773680; UTM 3116591]. In the next 650 meters the trail offers some great views off towards Baseseachi. The trail then begins to switchback up the mountain side [12R 0773334; UTM 3117188]. According to a sign on a tree it is 800 meters to the end of the trail.

Eventually the trail tops out at a Mirador offering great views of the Barranca Candamenia. The trail does continue on past this lookout point for about another 10 minutes to another great viewpoint overlooking Baseseachi Falls and the Barranca Candamenia to the north. **Exercise extreme caution here as there are no guard rails to protect people from the dangerous precipices.**

Route 43: Piedra Bolada Trail

Distance: 8 kilometers return
Time: 6 hours
Difficulty: Moderate
Hazards: High altitude; some loose rock on trail; altitude; last 150 meters of trail on a steep slope - boots recommended
Elevation Change: Climb 180 meters to second shelter; drop down 130 meters into Piedra Bolada canyon. Total altitude change is 310 meters
Topo Maps: H-12-D-89 San Isidor Huajumar
Attractions: Walk through pine and oak forests; walk along a smooth rock stream bed in the Piedra Bolada canyon; bathing pools along the stream; views of the top of Piedra Bolada falls and Barranca Candamania, bathing spots

The directions for this trial are the same as for Route 42 from Rancho San Lorenzo cabins to Shelter 2. From Shelter 2, take the left fork. The trail begins to drop immediately and swing to the right into the Piedra Bolada canyon. Note the red Lobo arrow signs pointing off in that direction. In about 10 minutes the trail passes a rock outcrop above the stream [12R 0773544; UTM 3116422]. The trail is a little vague over the rock but becomes distinct again on the other side of it. In another 10 minutes the trail passes by another rock outcrop to the left[12R 0773425; UTM 3116259]. It then drops over the rock outcrop and descends for about 50+ meters. It gets a little vague in the low shrubbery but look ahead for a red arrow nailed to a tree. Within another 50 meters the trail descends to the stream. There is a bit of a flat area here with a large rock cairn.

Walk past the cairn and pick up the trail again on the right-hand side of the stream. Walk along the right side of the stream for another 10 minutes or so. The trail then crosses the stream, then almost immediately crosses back over to the right side. [**Note**: Leave some kind of a marker here (red ribbon, rock cairn, pointing sticks, etc.) in order to recognize where to pick up the trail on your return. This point can be easily missed and you could find yourself hiking up the stream bed for quite a distance for nothing. Others have gone astray at this point. One couple spent an uncomfortable night out here while waiting to be rescued.

Within a few minutes the trail climbs a little above the stream. Look for two red Lobo arrows nailed to two different trees. One arrow points left. The other points straight on. Follow the arrow that points left. This trail parallels the stream for a few minutes, then drops down into the stream bed. From here on the stream is the trail. The stream bed is composed of reasonably smooth rock and is relatively easy walking. It's just a case of walking along the sides of the stream or rock hopping down the middle. We did this walk in early March when the flow was low. In higher water you might want to wear Tevas or water tennies to walk this portion. The trail along the stream bed continues on like this for another 20 minutes or so until you eventually come to a point where the stream drops steeply over a rock lip, veers off to the left and then drops down over another lip. This is a good spot to have a lunch, a rest and possibly a dip in one of the many pools along the stream.

About 100 meters back upstream, there is a small rock cairn on the left. This marks the trail which goes up and over a rock ridge. It's quite steep with loose rock making footing tricky. A good pair of hiking boots is required here. This part can be a bit dangerous so take your time and make sure your footing is secure. I would not attempt this if conditions were the least bit wet or slippery. Once achieving the top of the ridge [12R 0772547; UTM 3116033], you get a breathtaking view of the top of the falls and surrounding canyon lands. I advise against continuing on as the descent into the stream bed below is very steep and footing is loose making the trail very dangerous. The view from up here is about as good as it gets.

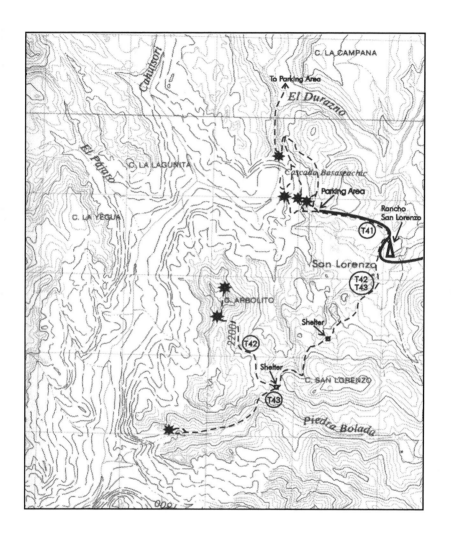

Further Reading

Burford, Tim. *Backpacking in Mexico*. The Globe Pequot Press Inc, USA, Old Saybrook, Connecticut,1997. ISBN: 1-898323-56-9

Conrad, Jim. *Mexico: A Hiker's Guide to Mexico's Natural History*. The Mountaineers, Seattle, Washington, 1995. ISBN: 0-89886-424-0

Mader, Ron. *Mexico: Adventures in Nature*. John Muir Publications, Santa Fe, New Mexico, 1998. ISBN: 1-56261-340-5

Church, Mike and Terry. *Traveler's Guide to Mexican Camping*. Rolling Homes Press, Livingston, TX, 2006. ISBN: 0-97494-712-9

Noble, John et al. *Mexico*. Lonely Planet Publications, Oakland, CA, 1998. ISBN: 0-86442-429-9

Cummings, Joe. *Northern Mexico Handbook: Including the Copper Canyon*. Moon Publications, Chico, CA, 1998. ISBN: 1-56691-118-4

Franz, Carl. *The People's Guide to Mexico*. John Muir Publications, Santa Fe, NM, 1994. ISBN: 1-56261-098-8

About the Author

Gerry was born and raised in the small village of Grand Marais on the east shore of Lake Winnipeg in Mamitoba, Canada. Surrounded by nature, Gerry developed a strong appreciation for the outdoors.

He is a member of the Manitoba Naturalists Society. He is an avid hiker, experienced canoeist and camper. He has hiked extensively in Canada, the U.S.. Mexico, South America, and Europe. He has participated in extended canoe trips on the many lakes and rivers in Canada's boreal forest as well as on several rivers and lakes in the Canadian Arctic. For the last ten years Gerry has been involved in securing and developing a 72 mile long abandoned rail line which runs north through Manitoba's interlake country. For four and a half years he was president of the Prime Meridian Trail Association.

Holding a Masters of Education degree, he has taught outdoor education classes. Because of his vast outdoor experience, he has collaborated with other outdoor groups and agencies in the development and promotion of hiking and canoeing.

In retirement he continues to be actively involved in hiking, cycling and canoeing. He and his wife Maureen have traveled to other parts of the world to seek out interesting and exotic places and trails. He has studied Spanish for several years and continues to improve his Spanish through reading, working with a tutor and traveling in Spanish speaking countries. Both he and Maureen have traveled extensively throughout Mexico in their truck camper over a period of ten years seeking out walking and hiking trails in Mexico's backcountry.